MAKING THINGS GREENER

Making Things Greener

Motivations and influences in the greening of manufacturing

MARDIE TOWNSEND
Deakin University
Australia

Studies
in
Green Research

Aldershot • Brookfield USA • Singapore • Sydney

Published by
Ashgate Publishing Ltd
Gower House
Croft Road
Aldershot
Hants GU11 3HR
England

Ashgate Publishing Company
Old Post Road
Brookfield
Vermont 05036
USA

British Library Cataloguing in Publication Data
Townsend, Mardie
    Making things greener : motivations and influences in the
    greening of manufacturing. - (Studies in green research)
    1. Industries - Environmental aspects 2. Manufacturing
    processes - Environmental aspects
    I. Title
    658.4'08

Library of Congress Catalog Card Number: 98-70992

ISBN 1 84014 385 1

658.408
T74m

Contents

List of Figures		*vii*
List of Tables		*viii*
Preface		*ix*
Acknowledgements		*x*
List of Abbreviations		*xi*

1	"Unless we Change we'll Get Where we're Going"	1
2	Human Behaviour Towards the Environment - Patterns and Understandings	7
3	'Green' Industry - Myth or Reality?	27
4	Structuration Theory - a Framework for Analysis of 'Green' Industry	34
5	Methodological Approach	47
6	Why Companies Go 'Green' - What the Literature Says	59
7	Motivations for the 'Greening' of Industry - 'Insider' Views	76
8	Help from Inside and Outside - Factors Assisting the 'Greening' of Industry	93
9	Hurdles and Hindrances - Factors Inhibiting the 'Greening' of Industry	116

10   A Typology of 'Green' Companies   156

11   Tips for Growing 'Greener' - Conditions Needed for
      'Green' Industry to Expand   178

Bibliography   *190*
Index   *198*

List of Figures

Figure 2.1   Ecocentrism and Technocentrism   22

Figure 5.1   Multiple Layers of Abductive Research   50

List of Tables

Table 2.1   Differences Between the Industrial and
             Post-industrial Paradigms   18
Table 5.1   Relevant Situations for Different Research
             Strategies   51
Table 7.1   Motivating Factors Influencing the 'Greening'
             of Industry   77
Table 8.1   Internal Factors Assisting the 'Greening' of
             Industry   94
Table 8.2   External Factors Assisting the 'Greening' of
             Industry   101
Table 9.1   Factors Hindering the 'Greening' of Industry   118

Preface

When I began the research on which this book is based, I was confronted by a great deal of cynicism. One wit commented: "Green industry? Well, that will be the shortest Ph.D. ever!" Others were more cutting, labelling the 'greening' of industry as a fraud or as a side benefit of cost cutting measures. But I was convinced that there *were* companies out there at least attempting to be ecologically sustainable in their manufacturing, and who were doing it for reasons other than just the bottom line. The key questions for me were: What factors other than financial benefits motivate companies to 'go green'? Why are some companies doing it when others are not? What factors help and hinder the 'greening' of industry? And how can the 'greening' of industry be fostered?

The past seven years have been a journey of discovery. In seeking answers to my questions, I have had the privilege of meeting and spending time with some amazing people. Their stories form the basis of this book. I came home often from my interviews with them, feeling a mixture of elation, excitement and frustration: elation, because I was one step closer to finding the answers to my questions; excitement, because I had been challenged by new ideas and concepts and had caught a glimpse of new possibilities; frustration, because the hurdles which were (and are) hindering these individuals and their companies in their attempts to be 'green' seemed (and still seem) so pointless and unnecessary.

As we approach the next millennium, there seems to be an unwillingness amongst governments, institutions, corporations and individuals to accept that the current 'Industrial Era' paradigm is ecologically unsustainable in even the short term, let alone in another thousand years. This book is written in the hope that people will see that it is not an impossible task for industry to become sustainable. It does not require us to do anything outrageous, but simply to make a commitment to an environmental ethic and to demonstrate that through practical actions. If we do this, the celebrations for the new millennium will truly begin!

Acknowledgements

I would like to acknowledge the support of many people who have helped me in the preparation of this book.

Both in Australia and overseas, many people and organisations have provided me with valuable background information, for which I am grateful. Special thanks go to the representatives of the companies included in this study, who so patiently and willingly gave of their time and their interest to provide me with information, to check the accuracy of my understandings and to update my information as circumstances changed.

Thanks are also due to Professor Norman Blaikie, who provided incisive comments and helpful advice at several key points of the research and during the writing process, and to my colleague, Mary Mahoney, who has encouraged and supported me during the preparation of this book.

But the two most heartfelt acknowledgements are reserved for my friend and colleague, Associate Professor Erica Hallebone, and for my family.

Erica has been a mentor since my first day of undergraduate study. Her inspiration, encouragement, friendship, humour, support, wisdom, patience, ready availability as an advisor and (most of all) her belief in me, have been unending.

To my family - Ron, Ruth, Joel and Paul - who have nagged me when I needed it; put me in my place when I seemed likely to go 'over the top', done my household chores, tolerated my 'absence', and boasted about my research and this book (so that I had no choice but to complete it), thank you. Without your support and belief, it would never have happened.

List of Abbreviations

ABS	Australian Bureau of Statistics
ACF	Australian Conservation Foundation
ACIC	Australian Chemical Industry Council
ACSMA	Australian Chemical Specialty Manufacturers' Association
AFCO	Australian Federation of Consumer Organisations
AMC	Australian Manufacturing Council
CDA	controlled droplet application
CEDA	Committee for Economic Development of Australia
CEO	Chief Executive Officer
CFL	compact fluorescent light bulb
CSIRO	Commonwealth Scientific & Industrial Research Organisation
EMDG	Export Market Development Grant (scheme)
EPA	Environment Protection Authority
ESD	Ecologically Sustainable Development
GDP	gross domestic product
HDPE	high density poly-ethylene
IBE	Institute of Business Ethics
IoD	(British) Institute of Directors
ISO	International Standards Organisation
ITES	International Trade Enhancement Scheme
NGO	non-governmental organisation
OPEC	Organisation of Petroleum Exporting Countries
PACIA	Plastics and Chemical Industries Association Inc.
PET	Polyethylene Tetephthalate
R & D	research and development
RETP	resource and energy throughput
RMIT	Royal Melbourne Institute of Technology
SECV	(former) State Electricity Commission of Victoria
UV	ultra-violet (radiation)
VEDC	Victorian Economic Development Corporation
WCED	World Commission on Environment and Development

1 "Unless we Change we'll Get Where we're Going"

Introduction

In 1991, when research for this book began, Australia (like many industrialised nations) was confronting serious problems, both economically and environmentally. Little has changed in the intervening years, and those problems remain evident today, affecting both urban and rural areas.

Economic problems, relating (at least in part) to the decline in manufacturing industry, have resulted in high levels of unemployment and a substantial foreign debt. According to the 1991 report of the Ecologically Sustainable Development (ESD) Working Group on Manufacturing (p.11), manufacturing then accounted for one-sixth of Australian production, employed over 1 million people and contributed $12 billion or one-fifth of total export revenue.

However, figures released in 1992 by the Australian Bureau of Statistics (ABS), showed that the percentage of GDP contributed by manufacturing industry declined from 26.2% in 1962-63 to 15.9% in 1989-90. (ABS 1992 p.142) Recent figures indicate that this has declined further, with manufacturing currently contributing just 13.8% of GDP. (ABS 1997)

In a report prepared for the Australian Manufacturing Council (AMC) in July 1990, Pappas, Carter, Evans & Koop/Telesis highlighted the importance of a strong manufacturing industry to the future economic well-being of Australia. The report of the ESD Working Group on Manufacturing (p.54) confirmed this, stating:

> the significance of manufacturing is enhanced by the need for all sectors to contribute to both the stabilisation of foreign debt and an improved current account, through increased exports and import replacement.

1

As well as confronting economic problems, over recent years Australia, along with the rest of the world, has experienced a growing awareness that global action needs to be taken promptly to overcome problems relating to bio-physical environmental damage. Charles Birch sums up the situation well:

> "Unless we change we'll get where we're going." (Anon., cited in Birch 1993 p.107)

It is the realisation of the essential truth of this statement in relation to the environment which has prompted some human beings to look at their patterns of behaviour and to try to discern new ways forward.

There is strong evidence that current patterns of human behaviour are unsustainable. The following excerpt from the report of the World Commission on Environment and Development (WCED) highlights the scope and the seriousness of the problem:

> Each year another 6 million hectares of productive dryland turns into worthless desert. ... More than 11 million hectares of forests are destroyed yearly. ... In Europe, acid precipitation kills forests and lakes and damages the artistic and architectural heritage of nations; it may have acidified vast tracts of soil beyond reasonable hope of repair. The burning of fossil fuels puts into the atmosphere carbon dioxide, which is causing gradual global warming. This 'greenhouse effect' may by early next century have increased average global temperatures enough to shift agricultural production areas, raise sea levels to flood coastal cities, and disrupt national economies. Other industrial gases threaten to deplete the planet's protective ozone shield to such an extent that the number of human and animal cancers would rise sharply and the oceans' food chain would be disrupted. Industry and agriculture put toxic substances into the human food chain and into the underground water tables beyond reach of cleansing. (WCED 1990 p.3)

Birch (1993 p.111), citing similar disasters, points out that "our present treatment of the Earth cannot continue for ever. The world is dying. We are on an unsustainable course".

Schmidheiny (1992 p.1) points to five important global trends underlying the unsustainable nature of current human existence: rapid human population growth; accelerating consumption of natural resources; accelerating environmental degradation; diminished biological diversity; and pollution of atmosphere, water and soil.

In Australia, as Dunkley (1992) notes, many of these trends are clearly evident. Salination or other forms of degradation afflict more than half of our farmland. Our extinction rate for mammals is the worst in the world, with 10% of our mammal species lost over the last 200 years - a rate five times greater than the global average. As well, during the same period, we have lost 97 species of plants, and a further 2000 plant species are classified as 'threatened'. We also have "the dubious distinction of being the world's second largest per capita producer of rubbish". (Dunkley p.29)

According to Winter (1988 p.11), on a global scale "industry is ... one of the prime causes of this damage, which is why industry is a prime target for attempts to improve the environmental situation".

Despite the Australian Government's stance at the recent Kyoto summit, there is increasing recognition that high levels of Greenhouse gas emissions, depletion of the ozone layer, pollution and resource depletion have undermined the ecological sustainability of Australia, and are also contributing to economic and health impacts.

As a result, at the same time as it is being asked to become more globally oriented and more competitive, Australian manufacturing industry is being challenged to improve its environmental performance. A report by the Committee for Economic Development of Australia (CEDA 1992 p.19) noted that "boardrooms have to deal with increasingly tougher standards, greater controls over land use and more severe penalties for environmental damage".

However, the same report went on to point out that this forced focus on environmental issues has its commercial benefits:

> One byproduct of environmental concerns has been the creation of opportunities for the development of environment management products and processes. (CEDA 1992 p.22)

For verification of this, one need look no further than the report entitled *Valuable export market opens for environmental technologies*, which appeared in the Financial Review on 17th August 1992. The report stated that:

> Australian environmental technologies and skills are actively being sought by foreign companies and could lead to the development of a multi-million dollar export market for Australian manufactured goods as well as services. (McKanna, 1992 p.55)

Suggestions have been put forward that the development of environmentally benign products and processes and the use of renewable energy sources would not only serve as a means of meeting these environmental needs, but could also contribute to a solution for our current economic woes.

The Commission of the European Communities' paper *European Competitiveness in the 21st Century* states:

> means of production and product ranges which improve the quality of life, safe-guard the environment and minimise waste material and energy will not only be vital for European society, but will also have commercial significance for export markets as these issues become a growing world-wide concern. (Cooley 1990 p.2)

Such potential is obviously not restricted to European industries. However, in order to gauge the extent of potential for Australia to develop environmentally preferred industries, information is required concerning the factors which motivate and facilitate the development of such industries.

The Focus of this Study

The socio-environmental literature on 'green' industry indicates that both internal and external factors influence company decision making. External factors include such things as market opportunity, regulatory frameworks, and financial constraints such as tariffs - what might be termed 'structural' influences.   Internal factors include both 'structural' factors, such as corporate decision making processes, access to capital and to appropriate technology, and 'cultural' factors, such as organisational culture, and the motivations, meanings and beliefs of management and staff.

It is accepted that most people who establish businesses do so with "the aim of making a reasonable profit" (Winter 1988 p.23). Yet, as Hawken (1993 p.xiii) points out:

> many companies today no longer accept the maxim that the business of business is business. Their new premise is simple: Corporations, because they are the dominant institution on the planet, must squarely address the social and environmental problems that afflict humankind.

By implication, of course, Hawken's statement indicates that many other companies do not respond in such socially and environmentally responsible ways. Leighton (1992 p.25) supports this view and points out that even many companies which claim to be acting with responsibility are in fact only dabbling in environmental improvement. Given the potential for an expansion of 'green' industry to contribute to the solution of many of Australia's problems at present, there is a need to understand the factors affecting the choice of some companies to adopt 'green' processes and produce 'green' products when other companies do not.

This book is based on case studies of Australian companies which, at the time the study commenced (1991), were producing environmentally preferred products and/or utilising ecologically sustainable processes in their manufacturing (commonly known as 'green' businesses). The research had as its objectives:

- to ascertain what other factors (apart from the profit motive) were involved in their decision to produce 'green' products and/or utilise 'green' processes;
- to identify the factors which have aided and hindered their development as 'green' businesses; and
- to identify the conditions needed to promote the development of further 'green' industries in Australia.

Definition of Terms

Throughout this book, a number of terms have been used to describe the products, processes, companies and industries investigated.

The general terms used include 'environmentally preferred', 'green', 'ecologically sustainable'. As this study has not involved any serious assessment of the environmental quality of the products or processes produced or used by the companies included in the sample, the use of these terms should not be interpreted as a verification of such quality.

Three different terms have been used to classify 'green' products, based on their impacts:

- 'Environmentally corrective' products are defined as those which help to reverse the negative impacts of environmental degradation caused by other products or processes. An example of an environmentally corrective product would be an oil-spill coagulant.
- 'Environmentally ameliorative' products are defined as those which allow humans to live with the lasting effects of environmental degradation. They include such products as UV protection equipment.
- 'Environmentally benign' products are defined as those which offer a less damaging alternative to products currently in use which are damaging to the environment. Such products include solar powered devices.

2 Human Behaviour Towards the Environment - Patterns and Understandings

The Influence of Attitudes and Values on Human Behaviour Towards the Environment

According to Barbour (1980 p.60), a value may be defined as "a general characteristic of an object or state of affairs that a person views with favour, believes is beneficial, and is disposed to act to promote". Barbour says:

> To hold a value is *to have a favourable attitude towards its realisation ....to believe that its realisation would be beneficial* ...(and) *to be disposed to act to promote its realisation.*

Rokeach (1973 p.7) expresses similar views, suggesting that "values ... have cognitive, affective, and behavioural components". According to Rokeach:

> A value is a cognition about the desirable ... is affective in the sense that (a person) can feel emotional about it, be affectively for or against it ... (and) has a behavioural component in the sense that it is an intervening variable that leads to action when activated.

Rokeach (1973 p.14) also highlights the motivational component of values, stating that they are "the conceptual tools and weapons that we all employ in order to maintain and enhance self-esteem".

The implications of this for 'green' industry are highlighted by Winter (1988 p.22). Winter, outlining reasons for an 'environmentalist' approach to business management, says:

> Without environmentalist business management, businessmen will be in conflict with their own consciences - and without self-respect, there can be no real sense of identification with one's job.

7

As Barbour (1980 p.61) points out, "values are not held in isolation but as components of *a value system,* a hierarchy, or ordered set". A value system may also be known by the term 'ethic', as Collins English Dictionary points out, defining an 'ethic' as "a moral principle or set of moral values held by an individual or group". (Hanks 1979 p.502) In a similar vein, Dobson (1990 p.47) describes ethics as "a code of conduct".

Leopold (1948 p.238) points to the importance of values and ethics in environmental behaviour by linking the philosophical understanding of the term 'ethic' with the ecological understanding of the same word:

> An ethic, ecologically, is a limitation on freedom of action in the struggle for existence. An ethic, philosophically, is a differentiation of social from anti-social conduct. These are two definitions of one thing.

Arguably, then, an 'environmental ethic' (a system of values which involves a favourable attitude toward the environment) will result in behaviour which limits impacts on the environment. This has important implications for any understanding of 'green' industry.

The hierarchical nature of values is also emphasised by Barbour (1980 p.61) who states:

> Basic values are those that are seldom subordinated to derivative values in cases of value conflict, and that serve as the criteria for justifying derivative values.

This approach is similar to that put forward by Abraham Maslow (1968), who defines a hierarchy of five levels of human need as a basis for the ordering of values. Barbour (1980) describes Maslow's hierarchy of human needs as follows:

- Survival (physiological needs): food, shelter, health.
- Security (safety needs): protection from danger and threat.
- Belonging (social needs): friendship, acceptance, love.
- Self-esteem (ego needs): self-respect, recognition, status.
- Self-actualisation (fulfilment needs): creativity, realisation of individual potentialities.

However, Barbour (1980 p.62), whilst describing Maslow's hierarchy of needs as "very helpful in any consideration of values", questions the implication that higher level needs only emerge when lower needs are satisfied.

Barbour's view is largely supported by the literature which demonstrates that environmentally protective business behaviour can be seen to meet a number of different levels of need at the same time: survival (in the sense of earning income), security (in reducing the threat of environmental disasters), self-esteem (as highlighted by Winter 1988), and self-actualisation (through the development of innovative products and services). Nevertheless, several notable exceptions have been identified in recent literature.

Worcester (1994) found a link between levels of human need and attitudes towards the environment in the United Kingdom, with increased levels of concern about environmental issues corresponding to declines in the level of and concern about inflation and unemployment.

Similarly, Mayer (1993 p.24), commenting on the outcomes of the British Institute of Directors' (IoD) 1993 survey of members, drew attention to the comment by the IoD that "the environment had slipped down or off the boardroom agenda because 'business has had to concentrate on its core activities purely to survive the recession'". Mayer (1993 p.24) went on to comment:

> The ramifications of that stance should not be overlooked. It suggests, for instance, that the environment may deserve attention during times of prosperity, but that such luxuries cannot be afforded in times of recession.

Other recent research into the impact of values on behaviour with regard to the environment (Karp 1996) has drawn on the work of Schwartz (1992), and in particular on Schwartz's "two-dimensional construct" (Karp 1996 p.130). In this construct:

> values are arrayed along two dimensions ... (The first is) a dimension of self-enhancement to self-transcendence ... (which) reflects the distinction between values oriented toward the pursuit of self-interest and values related to a concern for the welfare of others. ... The second dimension contrasts openness to change with conservation. ... This dimension indicates the degree to which individuals are motivated to independent action and willing to challenge themselves for both intellectual and emotional realisation. (Karp pp.113-114)

According to Karp (1996), where values of self-transcendence intersect with values of openness to change, pro-environmental behaviour is likely. By contrast, where values of self-enhancement intersect with values of conservation (in the sense of resistance to change), pro-environmental behaviour is unlikely.

It seems clear, then, that the attitudes and values held by individuals, and the activation of those values as intervening variables, will be important factors in the development of 'green' industry.

Organisational Theory and 'Behaviour'

To understand the 'greening' of industry, it is necessary to understand not only the factors affecting the behaviour of individuals, but also those affecting the companies (organisations) concerned.

The literature identifies a number of factors which impact on the 'behaviour' of organisations.

Organisational Culture

Beaumont et al. (1994 p.203) highlight the centrality of organisational culture to the structure and functioning of organisations, saying:

> culture should not be seen as something an organisation has, rather culture is what the organisation is.

Organisational culture entails a set of shared beliefs and values about the way the organisation should function. According to Beaumont et al. (p.204), it entails three key elements: material culture (the tangible expressions of the culture, such as buildings and other objects); attitudes and values; and "basic assumptions and core beliefs".

> The organisational culture contains values and basic assumptions, information about what the organisation is, about its mission and its *raison d'être*. (Beaumont et al. p.204)

According to Beaumont et al. (1994), the interaction which an organisation has with other organisations, and its dealings with stakeholders such as workers, shareholders, customers and suppliers, are all prescribed to a great extent by this organisational culture.

An important element in transformation in companies is change in the organisational culture. Beaumont et al. (1994 pp.205-206) cite the example of the UK transport sector:

> one sees the need for change, not only in investment but also in changing the attitudes of staff who have often lacked courtesy and have frequently seemed to view passengers as at best a nuisance. To change such deep-seated attitudes requires a shift in organisational culture - a creation of new myths.

Such a change is, according to Beaumont et al. (1994), very difficult to achieve and may take a significant period of time. They note, by contrast, the relative ease of changing business strategy and technology.

Another important aspect of organisational culture relevant to this study is its links with national culture which Beaumont et al. (1994 p.206) suggest is "an important driving force of corporate culture". They highlight the comments made by Webb (1991 p.1), who says:

> Two previous reports on environmental policies in France and Germany drew attention ... to the deeply distinctive understanding of what is meant by the environment, characteristic of each country.

Decision Making in Organisations

Another key issue within organisational theory which is directly relevant to this study is the process of decision making in organisations.

According to Jackson (1982 p.87), there is an inherent problem in considering the nature of organisational decision making: that of reification. Jackson points out that individuals, not organisations, make decisions.

In Jackson's view, the questions which need to be asked are 'who makes the decisions?' and 'who has the most influence over the decision making process?' This will vary according to the structure and culture of the organisation.

Denton (1994 p.98) distinguishes between the vertical approach to management in traditional organisations and the "flatter, more horizontal approach" which is often a feature of less traditional organisations. According to Denton, "delegating decision making downward ... gives everyone a sense of ownership and accountability". He goes on to point out the importance of shared decision making:

a case can be made that an exceptional CEO or group of highly talented vice-presidents can make very good decisions without (lower level worker) participation, but there's a high cost. People simply do not care! There are also strong reasons why as many need to participate as possible - regardless of the quality of the decision. High involvement by all levels, functions, and individuals creates a greater understanding of decisions by everyone. If you have ever been involved in the deciding, you know you are a lot more likely to be committed to implementing those decisions. After all, you have a stake in making it happen, plus you have a greater understanding of corporate (or otherwise) objectives. (Denton 1994 p.98)

As well as this emphasis on participatory decision making, however, Denton (1994 p.135) also emphasises the importance of leadership in companies, with clear policies being articulated and communicated throughout the organisation. Beaumont et al. (1994) support this view. Like Denton, they emphasise that for modern organisations a traditional hierarchical model of leadership, with an authoritarian head and strict rules and procedures, is inappropriate. They quote Henry Boettinger, who was formerly the Director of Corporate Planning, AT&T, to emphasise this point:

To manage is to lead, and to lead others requires that one enlists the emotions of others to share a vision as their own. (Boettinger in Beaumont et al. 1994 p.216)

The literature seems to suggest, therefore, that where there is a combination of clear (but not authoritarian) leadership and collective ownership of ideas, company decisions (such as decisions to adopt 'green' processes) are more likely to draw commitment from staff.

Organisations and their Environments

The interdependency of organisations and their environments is also a common theme in the literature, reflecting the importance of such relationships. For example, Shrivastava (1993 p.36) notes that "organisation-environment relations do not involve passive reactive interdependencies, but rather two-way mutual influences that sustain each other".

Mayo et al. (1995 p.75) also acknowledge these interdependencies, describing three levels at which organisational behaviour can be analysed to identify the "transactions (experience and action)" of the various unit types with their environments.

> The individual-in-organisation system involves the relationship between organisational members and their environment, which includes groups in which they work as well as the organisation as a whole and the sociocultural environment external to the organisation. The group-in-environment system involves those relationships between work groups and its more immediate environment, frequently the organisation. The organisation-in-environment system refers to the relationships between the organisation as a whole with its environment (eg. industry, competitors, government regulations).

They cite the study by Dutton and Dukerich (1991) of the Port Authority in New York as an example of a transactional study which identified the mutual influence of environment and organisation on one another over time.

> The (Port Authority's) building is situated in a place of increased numbers of homeless people. Homelessness was a major problem for the organisation in 1982. It was treated as a police security issue. At that time, the organisation's identity was one of a professional organisation ill suited to social service activities. However, the loss of image of the organisation as a consequence of removing the homeless by enforcing anti-loitering laws (it was called 'the nightmare of 42nd Street') led the company to change its strategy, and at the same time it changed the identity and image of its members. The authors were able to identify five marked phases in the development of the corporate issue, namely: homelessness as a police security issue, as a corporate issue (but this company is not involved in social service), as a business problem and moral, as an image problem (no one else will deal with it), and as an issue of competitiveness. The Homeless Project Team was created at the initiative of the Port Authority to help homeless people. Their involvement with the homeless is now a major part of the Port Authority organisation. (Mayo et al. 1995 p.85)

Shrivastava (1993 p.31) asserts that there is an important element omitted from the decision making frameworks of many companies: the acknowledgement of the relevance of the physical environment to their activities.

> Management theory and practice have adopted a peculiarly distorted definition of organisational environment. They erroneously view organisational environment as all economic, social, political, technological and commercial forces that influence the organisational performance. .... This definition is biased towards economic performance and economistic thinking. It ignores the fact that 'nature' is the most fundamental environment of all human and consequently all organisational activities.

Detailed discussion on factors influencing the decisions of companies to adopt environmentalist policies and practices is included below.

Historical Overview of Attitudes and Behaviour Towards the Environment

According to Barbour (1980 p.13), human beings' treatment of the environment is a reflection of our "broad cultural assumptions about nature". Three broad classifications of attitudes to nature are presented by Barbour (1980 p.13): "Domination over Nature, Unity with Nature, and Stewardship of Nature (intermediate between the first two positions)".

Birch (1993 p.92) uses a similar classification, but applies different terms: for the term 'domination' he substitutes 'exploitation', and for 'unity' he uses the term 'compassion'. Birch goes on to reflect on the way such attitudes relate to human valuation of nature:

> In exploitation we ascribe only instrumental value to non-human creatures. While stewardship adds an element of responsibility, it still ascribes no more than instrumental value to non-human creatures. Only the third attitude (compassion) ascribes intrinsic value to nature ... .

According to Barbour (1980 p.13):

> attitudes toward nature involve fundamental beliefs and values that have far reaching consequences ... (which) are correlated with distinctive attitudes toward resources, technology, and growth.

Since its beginnings in the Industrial Revolution, industry has had a reputation for exploiting the environment rather than protecting it.

Barbour (1980 p.1) notes that "for 200 years U.S. industrial growth has been propelled by cheap fuel, abundant resources and an environment that seemingly could absorb unlimited wastes".

The Industrial Era Paradigm

This approach is part of "the industrial era paradigm", of which the key features are said to be:

> expectation of unlimited material progress and ever-growing consumption; faith in science and technology to solve all problems; goals of efficiency, growth, and productivity; mastery of nature; and competition and individualism. (Barbour 1980 p.310)

As the features of the paradigm suggest, this approach is based on an attitude of domination over nature. Pepper (1984) describes this paradigm as 'technocentric'.

Barbour (1980) identifies a number of factors involved in the development of the dominant attitude of humans over nature. They include: Judaeo-Christian beliefs; the rise of the scientific world view in the 17th Century; the "American experience" (of pioneering and exploration); and the gender-based division of society.

Barbour (p.14) suggests that the Judaeo-Christian belief (as expressed in Genesis Ch.1, v.26-28) in "the separation of humanity and nature and the rights of humanity over nature" is a major source of environmentally destructive attitudes. Birch agrees that Western Christian thinking is based on an assumption of the absolute rule of humans over nature. However, he highlights the fact that it is the "anthropocentric exegesis" of this text, not the content of the text itself, which fostered the attitude that humans can, with impunity, treat nature as they please. (Birch 1993 p.93)

According to Barbour (1980), the rise of the scientific world view in the 17th Century provided further support for the domination of nature by humans. Birch supports this view, blaming first Greek culture, and later Descartes and Bacon, for fostering the dominant attitude already kindled through the anthropocentric interpretation of Old Testament scripture. This attitude arose particularly during the period of the Enlightenment, which Ronan describes as "the movement which looked on the world with a new rationalism that to a greater or lesser extent severed any connection between the natural world and God's continuing concern with it". (Ronan 1983 pp.399-400) Diespecker (1989 p.433), too, acknowledges the importance of the scientific world view in human interaction with the environment. He says: the "reductionist and mechanistic attitude toward ourselves and the universe" promoted by Cartesian-Newtonian science "has enabled us to progress and to evolve, but it has also imperilled life on Earth".

It is possible also that the imperialist nature of European society during the period of the 15th to the 19th Centuries may have contributed to attitudes towards nature and the environment. Barbour (1980 p.16) suggests that the experience of the American pioneers may have contributed to an attitude of domination over nature. He says:

> As the pioneers moved progressively westward, much that they encountered was hostile, a threat to survival, an obstacle to be overcome.

Australian history indicates that the white settlers here had no less to contend with, so it seems likely that the same might apply to them also. However, it is probable that the attitudes of the societies which the pioneers left were as important as the experiences provided by the lands to which they came, in forming their attitudes towards the environment. Those societies were imperialist in nature - seeking to conquer and subdue the peoples and lands which they 'discovered', and to acquire for their own benefit the resources of those new territories. This fostered not only a dominant attitude towards the environment, but also an exploitative one. This is reflected in Australia's history, with gold mining forming a major focus for development during the mid 19th century, and recent export figures indicating that over the last decade mining products have averaged over 25% of all exports. (Australian Bureau of Statistics 1992)

The attitude of environmental exploitation can also be linked to gender divisions within society. Barbour (1980 p.17) argues that "male-dominated society has admired in public life the aggressive, competitive, rational qualities that it calls 'masculine', rather than the nurturing, conserving, intuitive qualities that it associates with women and family life". He goes on to assert that "the exclusion of women from positions of economic and political power and the separation of the realms of work and home have accentuated this polarity". (Barbour 1980 p.17)

The inference, that women in general are more concerned than men about environmental issues, is accurate according to an Australian National Opinion Polls survey conducted late in 1992. The survey found that 'urban brownies' - people who take up the fight against urban environmental problems such as air pollution, over-development, and urban waste - are more likely to be women than men. It also found that "women with young children, in particular, rated the environment a priority issue". (Kelly 1993) It is not surprising, therefore, that male-dominated societies are often also societies in which the prevailing attitudes towards nature and the environment are also those of domination.

The Post-industrial/Environmental Paradigm

Recent years have seen the beginnings of "a paradigm shift", which Barbour (1980 p.310) explains as "a broader change in assumptions and perceptions". The key differences between the two paradigms are summed up in Table 2.1. The new "post-industrial paradigm" features:

> material sufficiency in the satisfaction of basic needs; frugality in resource use and transition to renewable resources; ecological ethics and stewardship of nature; goals of human development, self-realisation, and growth in awareness and creativity; and co-operation and community solidarity, in place of competition and individualism. (Barbour 1980 p.310)

A number of factors have been identified as contributing to the development of the new environmental paradigm. These include:

* increased information about environmental problems;
* the decline in competing social problems;
* increased threat posed by technological developments;
* more leisure leading to greater contact with the environment; and
* the growth of the counter-culture.

Sandbach (1980 p.1) stated:

> Without doubt historians of the future will regard the late 1960s and early 1970s as a period when most industrially developed countries became deeply concerned about environmental problems.

Contributing to this concern was an increased environmental awareness, prompted by the writings of people such as Rachel Carson and Paul Ehrlich, and by the events of the time:

during the 1960s a series of horror stories was revealed. Notably, there was the alleged death of Lake Erie, killed by excessive eutrophication resulting from pollution. There was the *Torrey Canyon* incident in March 1967, and there was the Japanese Minimata tragedy following mercury poisoning of fish. (Sandbach 1980 p.30)

Table 2.1:   Differences Between the Industrial and Post-industrial Paradigms

	Dominant (industrial) paradigm	Alternative (post-industrial) environmental paradigm
Core values	Material (economic growth)	Non-material (self-actualisation)
	Natural environment valued as a resource	Natural environment intrinsically valued
	Domination over nature	Harmony with nature
Economy	Market forces	Public interest
	Risk and reward	Safety
	Differentials	Egalitarian
	Individual self-help	Collective/social provision
Polity	Authoritative structures: experts influential	Participative structures: citizen/worker participation
	Hierarchical	Non-hierarchical
	Law and order	Liberation
Society	Centralised	Decentralised
	Large-scale	Small-scale
	Associational	Communal
	Ordered	Flexible
Nature	Ample reserves	Earth's resources limited
	Nature hostile/neutral	Nature benign
	Environment controllable	Nature delicately balanced
Knowledge	Confidence in science & technology	Limits to science & technology
	Rationality of means	Rationality of ends
	Separation of fact/value, thought/feeling	Integration of fact/value, thought/feeling

Source: Cotgrove, 1982 p.27

At the same time, "competing social problems such as poverty, housing and racial tension became less serious in the affluent post-Second World War period". (Sandbach 1980 p.32) In keeping with Maslow's hierarchy of needs hypothesis, Sandbach suggests that this decline in competing lower order social problems allowed attention to be focused on environmental concerns.

The pervasiveness of environmental problems resulting from modern technology, and the threat posed by technology 'out of control', increased the level of environmental concern. Barbour (1980 p.42) states:

> Events since World War II, however, have contributed to more widespread *anxiety about technology*. The destructiveness of the atom bomb dwarfed any previous human act, and the threat of nuclear annihilation has continued to hang over nations with missiles poised for launching.

Sandbach (1980 p.36) says:

> Nuclear fallout, oil pollution from the *Torrey Canyon*, and pesticides in food were all problems that could not be avoided by geographical mobility, as had been the case with many of the older and more local problems arising from slums, smoke and sewage.

Barbour (1980 p.44) points out that "we speak of 'runaway technology' as if it were a vehicle out of control, with a momentum that cannot be stopped".

In addition, Sandbach points out, increased leisure time and affluence since the Second World War have resulted in people having greater contact with the environment.

> In America, for example, the numbers of people visiting National Parks increased from 33.2 million in 1950 to 150.8 million in 1968, an increase of 450 per cent. Such changes ... made environmental concern a much more relevant policy issue. (Sandbach 1980 pp.36-37)

Both Sandbach and Barbour also highlight the influence of the counter-culture - the 'hippie' and 'youth culture' of the late 1960s and early 1970s - on the environmentalist movement. Barbour (1980 p.46) points out that:

(although) the counterculture that emerged in the late 1960s and early 1970s was never a unified movement, and many of its expressions were shortlived (nevertheless) ... some of its characteristic attitudes, including disillusionment with technology, have continued among a significant portion of the younger generation.

This view is supported by Blaikie and Ward (1992 p.42):

Youth in the late 1960s and early 1970s appear to be the age cohort which developed a high level of commitment, as a result of the attention which environmental issues received at that time, and they appear to have maintained something of this commitment, or to have responded favourably to the 'second wave' of environmental consciousness in the late 1980s.

However, it is important to acknowledge that, although there may be a correlation between a particular era and a particular paradigm and attitude toward nature, this is by no means exclusive. As Barbour (1980 p.13) points out, "in both the past and the present, attitudes toward nature have been extremely diverse".

For example, the idea of unity with nature is shared by the modern 'deep ecology' movement, as well as the Romanticists of the 18th and 19th centuries, and past and present native American culture. (Barbour 1980)

Other Recent Trends in Environmental Attitudes and Behaviour

A distinction is made, by Dobson (1990 p.13), between 'environmentalism', which he sees as "a 'managerial' approach to environmental problems" (exemplified by the new environmental paradigm), and 'ecologism', which (he says) "argues that care for the environment ... presupposes radical changes in our relationship with it, and thus in our mode of social and political life". Dobson's statement that:

Ecologism ... (goes) beyond human-instrumental reasons for care for the natural world, arguing that the environment has an independent value that should guarantee its 'right to life' (Dobson 1990 p.20)

indicates that ecologism clearly fits more comfortably with the third attitude toward nature identified by both Barbour (1980) and Birch (1993): that of 'unity' (Barbour's term) or 'compassion' (the term used by Birch).

Pepper (1986), in his analysis of 'environmentalism', based on the work of O'Riordan, accepts a broader definition of 'environmentalism' than that adopted by Dobson, citing the definition provided by the Dictionary of Human Geography (Johnston 1981):

The ideologies and practices which inform and flow from a concern with the environment.

As Figure 2.1 indicates, Pepper uses O'Riordan's classifications of 'technocentrism' and 'ecocentrism' in his analysis of environmentalism; but like Dobson he distinguishes between individuals who accord nature an intrinsic value and those who see only its instrumental value.

The 'deep ecology' movement, based on the writings of Arne Naess, is generally accepted as an example of 'ecologism' as distinct from 'environmentalism'. 'Deep ecology' is based on the following eight principles:

1. The flourishing of human and nonhuman life on Earth has inherent value. The value of nonhuman lifeforms is independent of the usefulness of the nonhuman world for human purposes.
2. Richness and diversity of life forms are also values in themselves and contribute to the flourishing of human and nonhuman life on Earth.
3. Humans have no right to reduce this richness and diversity except to satisfy vital needs.
4. The flourishing of human life and cultures is compatible with a substantial decrease of human population. The flourishing of nonhuman life requires such a decrease.
5. Present human interference with the nonhuman world is excessive and the situation is rapidly worsening.
6. Policies must therefore be changed. The changes in policies affect basic economic, technological, and ideological structures. The resulting state of affairs would be deeply different from the present and make possible a more joyful experience of the connectedness of all things.
7. The ideological change is mainly that of appreciating *life quality* (dwelling in situations of inherent value) rather than adhering to an increasingly higher standard of living. There will be a profound awareness of the difference between big and great.
8. Those who subscribe to the foregoing points have an obligation, directly or indirectly, to participate in the attempt to implement the necessary changes. (Naess 1985 in Milbrath 1989 p.161)

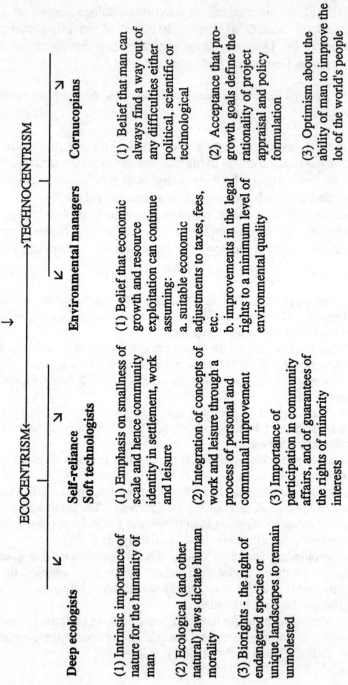

ENVIRONMENTALISM

ECOCENTRISM ←————————————→ TECHNOCENTRISM

Deep ecologists

(1) Intrinsic importance of nature for the humanity of man

(2) Ecological (and other natural) laws dictate human morality

(3) Biorights – the right of endangered species or unique landscapes to remain unmolested

Self-reliance Soft technologists

(1) Emphasis on smallness of scale and hence community identity in settlement, work and leisure

(2) Integration of concepts of work and leisure through a process of personal and communal improvement

(3) Importance of participation in community affairs, and of guarantees of the rights of minority interests

Environmental managers

(1) Belief that economic growth and resource exploitation can continue assuming:
a. suitable economic adjustments to taxes, fees, etc.
b. improvements in the legal rights to a minimum level of environmental quality

Cornucopians

(1) Belief that man can always find a way out of any difficulties either political, scientific or technological

(2) Acceptance that pro-growth goals define the rationality of project appraisal and policy formulation

(3) Optimism about the ability of man to improve the lot of the world's people

(4) Lack of faith in modern large-scale technology and its associated demands on elitist expertise, central state authority and inherently anti-democratic institutions

(5) Implication that materialism for its own sake is wrong and that economic growth can be geared to providing for the basic needs of those below subsistence levels

Participation seen both as a continuing education and political function

(4) Lack of faith in modern large-scale technology and its associated demands on elitist expertise, central state authority and inherently anti-democratic institutions

(5) Implication that materialism for its own sake is wrong and that economic growth can be geared to providing for the basic needs of those below subsistence levels

c. compensation arrangements satisfactory to those who experience adverse environmental and/or social effects

(2) Acceptance of new project appraisal techniques and decision review arrangements to allow for wider discussion or genuine search for consensus among representative groups of interested parties

(4) Faith that scientific and technological expertise provides the basic foundation for advice on matters pertaining to economic growth, public health and safety

(5) Suspicion of attempts to widen basis for participation and lengthy discussion in project appraisal and policy review

(6) Belief that all impediments can be overcome given a will, ingenuity and sufficient resources arising out of growth

Figure 2.1: Ecocentrism and Technocentrism
Source: Adapted from Pepper, 1986, based on O'Riordan, 1981

Other recent developments in environmentalism include the growth of eco-feminism and the development of the Gaia hypothesis.

Ecofeminism, which arose through the conjunction of the feminist movement and the environment movement in the late 1970s and early 1980s, has much in common with 'deep ecology' (otherwise known as 'transpersonal ecology'), as Eckersley (1992 pp.63-64) points out:

> Like transpersonal ecology, ecofeminism also proceeds from a process oriented, relational image of nature and seeks mutualistic social and ecological relationships based on a recognition of the interconnectedness, interdependence, and diversity of all phenomena.
>
> However, unlike transpersonal ecology, ecofeminism has taken the historical/symbolic association of women with nature as demonstrating a special convergence of interests between feminism and ecology. The convergence is seen to arise, in part, from the fact that patriarchal culture has located women somewhere between men and the rest of nature on a conceptual hierarchy of being (ie., God, Man, Woman, Nature). This has enabled ecofeminists to identify what they see as a similar logic of domination between the destruction of nonhuman nature and the oppression of women.

According to Young (1991), the 'Gaia Hypothesis', proposed by British scientist James Lovelock in 1979, arose from the work of scientists investigating the possibility of life on Mars and Venus.

> The paradoxical result of discovering that both planets were dead was the awesome realisation that the ability of the earth to support life was, in this solar system at least, unique. (Young 1991 p.121)

In attempting to explain the homeostasis of Earth, Lovelock developed the notion of 'Gaia', "suggesting that all earth elements (soil, water, air, plants, animals, minerals) are united into one interdependent entity". (Milbrath 1989 p.158)

Young (1991 p.122) puts it this way:

> once life was established, the biosphere continued to act as a self-regulating entity with the capacity to keep itself healthy by controlling the chemical and physical composition of the oceans, the atmosphere and the soil. ... Living things do not evolve, it seems, according to fixed laws in a dead world, but in living circumstances which, as living things, they help shape.

The implications of this for human behaviour are obvious, as Lovelock (1988 p.177) indicates:

> It follows that, if the world is made unfit by what we do, there is the probability of a change in regime to one that will be better for life, but not necessarily better for us.

The Likelihood of a Shift to an Ecological Paradigm

Dunkley (1992 p.118) outlines the value shifts which would be required for an 'ecologism' paradigm (my term) - a paradigm in keeping with the 'unity with nature' attitude - to become dominant:

- from competitiveness to co-operativeness;
- from egoism to altruism;
- from anthropocentrism to ecocentrism;
- from struggle against Nature to harmony with Nature;
- from individualism to social consciousness (without excluding the possibility of personal fulfilment);
- from male dominance to equal participation of women's perspectives (what some call 'feminisation', though not all feminists see it this way);
- from acquisitiveness to simplicity, or what has been called 'conspicuous frugality' (Brown, 1981 p.356ff);
- from consumerism to a concern primarily with basic needs; and
- more broadly, we require a re-definition of 'living standards' so as to break the nexus between income and incentives, and to counteract our obsession with productivity and economic growth. (Dunkley 1992 p.118)

To many people, there will appear to be little difference between the post-industrial/environmental paradigm and an 'ecologist' paradigm. However, according to Dobson (1990 p.36), the differences are clear.

> Ecologists and environmentalists are both inspired to act by the environmental degradation they observe, but their strategies for remedying it differ wildly. Environmentalists do not necessarily subscribe to the limits to growth thesis, nor do they typically seek to dismantle 'industrialism'. They are unlikely to argue for the intrinsic value of the non-human environment and would baulk at any suggestion that we (as a species) require 'metaphysical reconstruction' (Porritt, 1986 pp.198-200). Environmentalists will typically believe that technology can solve the problems it creates, and will probably regard any suggestions that only

'frugal living' will provide for sustainability as wilful nonsense.

Using Dobson's definitions, the companies examined in this study can be said to be clearly 'environmentalist' rather than 'ecologist', since they have a 'green' focus but are operating within the current social, political and economic framework of Australian society.

3   'Green' Industry - Myth or Reality?

The Relationship between Economics and Environment

The interrelationship between economics and the environment is often misunderstood. According to the ESD Working Group on Manufacturing:

> it is now widely accepted that economic activities affect the environment, often adversely. That the economy, in return, is dependent upon the integrity of the environment is, however, less readily understood. (1991 p.2)

However, recent literature indicates that this is changing - that there is a growing awareness of this interdependence throughout the global community.

The Committee for Economic Development of Australia (CEDA 1992 p.13) acknowledges that "long term growth and environmental protection are mutually dependent". A similar view is expressed by Brundtland, who says:

> the 'environment' is where we all live; and 'development' is what we all do in attempting to improve our lot within that abode.   The two are inseparable.   (WCED 1990 p.xv)

Zarsky (1990 p.27) reinforces this view, stating:

> improvements in material well-being, including increases in real income, need not come at the expense of environmental degradation. Indeed, unless economic decisions are ecologically rational, we will be unable to maintain, let alone improve, living standards.

Winter (1988 p.17) not only acknowledges the links between economics and the environment, but points to the implications of that link for industry. He states:

Year in, year out, environmental damage causes financial losses on a stupendous scale in Europe, along with the destruction of irreplaceable resources whose value cannot be expressed in money terms. ... This is the challenge which industry is facing: to restore the environment with the same panache with which the European economy was rebuilt after the Second World War. ... This challenge can only be met on the basis of an environmentalist approach to business management, which for a variety of reasons is also in the firms' own immediate interest.

This realisation of the interrelationship between economics and the environment has resulted in a new development in economic theory - environmental economics. Bennett (1991 p.2) says:

Rather than a paradox existing between economics and the environment, ... economics can provide a paradigm for environmentalism.
   The essence of the paradigm is that market forces can be harnessed to ensure the stewardship of the environment.

It is this proposition which forms the basis of the concept of 'ecologically sustainable development'.

The Concept of Sustainable ('Green') Industry

According to Birch (1993 p.113), the concept of ecologically sustainable development (ESD) had its origins at a World Council of Churches conference in Bucharest in 1974. The topic of the conference was 'science, technology and human development'.
   The original term used - ecologically sustainable society - meant "the society that could persist indefinitely into the future because it sustained the ecological base on which society is utterly dependent". (Birch 1993 p.114)
   In the 1987 report of the World Commission on Environment and Development (WCED), the term 'ecologically sustainable society' was changed to 'ecologically sustainable development' (ESD). This has since become the common usage.
   ESD has been defined as:

a process of change in which the exploitation of resources, the direction of investments, the orientation of technological development, and institutional change are all in harmony and enhance both current and future potential to meet human needs and aspirations. (WCED 1987 p.90)

Birch (1993 p.115) puts forward the argument (based on ideas derived from Daly 1991) that the term 'sustainable development' is misleading, since it implies economic growth:

but sustainable growth is an impossibility. Sustainable development makes sense for the economy only if it is understood as development without growth, that is a qualitative improvement of the economic base without an ever-increasing throughput of energy and other resources.

Dunkley (1992 p.3) also criticises the concept of ESD. He describes the "current fashion of seeking to reconcile environment and economics through new models of 'sustainable development' " as "flawed". He argues that the basic premises on which ESD is based:

i. that markets can facilitate the necessary adjustments; ii. that technological solutions will normally be found; iii. that resource and energy throughput (RETP) can be 'decoupled' from output ... , meaning that certain technologies will enable output to grow without greatly increasing RETP. (Dunkley 1992 p.20)

are problematic.

How 'Green' is 'Green Industry'?

The degree to which the post-industrial paradigm has become dominant is open to debate. Leighton (1992) agrees with the notion of a paradigm shift, describing it as the opening of a gate through which the world rushes. However, in terms of business and industry rushing through the gate of environmentalism, Leighton (1992 p.26) suggests that, to date, companies have only really:

dabbled in environmental improvement. They have done the easy things (like reducing packaging and buying recycled office paper), the pressing things (like eliminating the most carcinogenic substances from their operations and products) and the things that are costly in the short run but profitable in the long run (like new manufacturing processes that create less waste).

Leighton (1992 p.27) goes on to say that the time has now come for companies to move on "beyond the easy, the obvious, and the profitable to the next plateau of commitment".

This view is supported by Plant and Albert (1991 p.3), who distinguish between:

> shades of green business - 'light green' indicating a superficial, often profit-dictated, short-term response, while 'deep green' might stand for the more authentic attempts at dealing with the profound problem of humankind finding a genuinely sustainable way of inhabiting the planet into the long-term future.

Plant and Albert (1991) criticise green business not so much because of what it *does*, but because of what it *does not* achieve. Green business (they say) is, after all, "the proverbial motherhood ... : how could one *not* be green, and buy green ...?" Their criticism is that:

> most green business is, in essence superficial. For the production of environmentally friendly goods doesn't address the major structural and institutional obstacles in the way of an authentic greening of industrial society. (Plant & Albert 1991 p.4)

Similar 'ecologist' views are expressed by Dunkley (1992 p.2) who says:

> many social inequities and environmental problems are due fundamentally to the socially and ecologically unsustainable nature of industrial capitalism, and so cannot be cured without drastic change.

In a similar vein, according to an article by Schumpeter which appeared on page 4 of *The Age* 'Environment Supplement' on Wednesday 10th June 1992, "the Environmental Choice program has been labelled a 'greenwash' by consumer groups". The article goes on to state:

> The Australian Federation of Consumer Organisations (AFCO), the peak body for consumer groups, and the Australian Conservation Foundation are

both disappointed that Environmental Choice does not focus on each product's 'cradle-to-grave' impact on the environment.

Instead, to get the scheme's stamp of approval manufacturers will need only to highlight a single aspect of a product as in some way being environmentally advantageous, regardless of other characteristics of the product that may be detrimental to the environment. (Schumpeter 1992 p.4)

West (1995) highlights the problems associated with most (if not all) of the ecolabelling schemes around the world. These include:

- the failure to ensure that bodies making decisions on the types of products to which ecolabelling will apply and the criteria for assessing applications for ecolabels are truly independent of industry;
- the weakness of standards used by such schemes (which is a direct reflection of the influence of industry lobbying); and
- the narrowing and manipulation of the categories of products which are assessed under such schemes.

For example, according to West:

European light bulb manufacturers have fought hard to keep compact fluorescent light bulbs from being lumped into the same ecolabelling category as standard incandescent light bulbs - on the grounds that they do not perform the same functions. Compact fluorescent light bulbs (CFLs) are estimated to be six times as energy efficient as standard incandescent bulbs, yet standard incandescent bulbs account for over 90 per cent of the European market. Creating two separate product categories, one for CFLs and one for incandescent bulbs, resulting in two ecolabels, prevents consumers from comparing products and from making a broader environmental choice. (1995 p.18)

Therefore, West asserts:

At best, ecolabelling is a means of bringing about small incremental changes in product and production environmental standards which address a narrow definition of environmental impacts, based mainly on physical and material inputs and outputs. At worst, it is nothing more than a marketing gimmick. (1995 p.20)

The claims of businesses listed in the Green Directory 1992 are equally unproven. According to the Department of Small Business, "publication of the Green Directory is consistent with the Victorian Government's Conservation Strategy and in particular with the Government's goals of ensuring sustainable use of renewable resources, the wise use of non-renewable resources, maintaining essential ecological processes, preserving genetic diversity, and protecting natural resources". (Department of Small Business 1992) However, a disclaimer at the front of the Directory states:

> Listings of firms, products, services or information in this directory are based on information supplied by the businesses and are not necessarily approved, endorsed, accredited or supported by the Department of Small Business.

The report of the ESD Working Group on Manufacturing (1991 p.57) highlights the tendency for industry to fall short of its 'green' objectives. It states:

> An ecologically sustainable manufacturing sector must address both its production processes and the products it markets. In an ideal world manufacturing operations would create no environmental or health problems during the production process or through the use and disposal of the products. A more realistic vision of sustainable manufacturing might incorporate manufacturing processes:
>
> • which use the best environmental practices including the best technology from both environmental and economic perspectives;
> • where all opportunities are taken to minimise waste by extracting and collecting useful by-products from wastes where economically and technologically feasible;
> • where every attempt would be made to minimise or eliminate the production of hazardous waste and to dispose of it in ways that minimise environmental damage;
> • which, where possible, use renewable energy forms or less polluting sources of energy, and use all energy efficiently; and
> • which contribute to development of environmental technologies and products.

Plant and Albert (1991 p.3) suggest that much of what purports to be green business is a "hoax", and that:

in this age of highly sophisticated media manipulation, the public relations *image* that can be portrayed is far more important from a marketing point of view than the actual *content*. To *appear* to be green is the important (and profitable) thing.

However, an article by MacKenzie (1991) focusing on the emergence of the 'green consumer' indicates that industry has, to date, been less than successful in its promotion of itself as 'green'. According to MacKenzie (1991), uncertainty in the minds of consumers about the environmental claims made for products exacerbates an existing lack of trust in manufacturers. MacKenzie says:

> lack of confidence in manufacturers goes some way to explaining the suspicions attached to the environmental claims they make, and to the feeling that manufacturers are unlikely ever to be doing enough about environmental issues. ... the building back of trust in manufacturers would appear to be important ..in surmounting the barriers to further involvement in environmentally-friendly products. (1991 p.74)

4 Structuration Theory - a Framework for Analysis of 'Green' Industry

Introduction to the Theoretical Framework for the Study

As much as they are a challenge to science and technology, environmental problems are a challenge to social, economic and political structures and understandings. Environmental problem solving is therefore as much a social and political task as it is a technical and scientific one. As Lindblom (1985, in WCED 1990 p.386) states:

> The problems of today do not come with a tag marked energy or economy or CO_2 or demography, nor with a label indicating a country or a region. The problems are multi-disciplinary and transnational or global.
> The problems are not primarily scientific and technological. In science we have the knowledge and in technology the tools. The problems are basically political, economic, and cultural.

Dickens (1992 p.1) concurs with this sentiment, saying:

> There can be little doubt that the causes of contemporary ecological and environmental problems are largely associated with social relations, social pressures and political institutions.

This study, therefore, focuses on the sociological aspects of the greening of business, in the hope that the results may contribute to the resolution of environmental problems afflicting our planet and threatening our future.

The diverse nature of environmental problems - global and local, societal and individual - and the diversity of interpretations of those problems, highlights the need for an analytical framework which is particularly robust.

A range of social theories was examined in an attempt to identify one which would provide a comprehensive framework for the analysis of this issue.   Although no theory was identified which provided an *environmental* sociology framework including an integration of both structural and interpretive approaches, macro- and micro-sociological understandings, a theory was identified which did address the structural-interpretive/macro-micro dichotomies and which appeared to be sufficiently robust to enable its application to environmental sociology. According to Ritzer (1988 p.487), Giddens' structuration theory offers "perhaps the best known and the most articulated effort to integrate micro and macro concerns".   Dickens (1992) also points to the potential for Giddens' work to be applied to environmental sociology.

Structuration theory, therefore, provides the theoretical framework for this analysis of green industry.

The Issue of the Relationship between Structure and Agency

The growing awareness of the need to develop an understanding of human social behaviour which takes account of both the individual action involved in behaviour and the environment (both the socially constrained and constructed environment, and the natural environment) within which it takes place highlights a gap in existing sociological thought.

One could postulate a 'spectrum' of sociological perspectives or theories. At one end of the 'spectrum' have been the explanations provided by 'structural-functionalist' perspectives, which included originally functionalist theory and conflict (or Marxian) theory and more recently neo-Marxian theory and other non-Marxian conflict theories. These approaches have focused on the ways in which social structures direct or influence human behaviour. At the other end of the 'spectrum' there have been the explanations provided by 'social action' or 'interpretivist' perspectives which include Weberian social theory, symbolic interactionism, phenomenology and ethnomethodology. These perspectives focus on the ways in which society is created predominantly by humans' own actions and the meanings they ascribe to them.

The distinction between the two broad approaches is not clear cut, with most sociological perspectives attempting to address the issues of both structure and agency to some extent. However, most fail to do so adequately, tending either to focus on one level of analysis at the expense of the other or to simply offer separate and distinct applications of the different perspectives to a particular social problem.

Theories which focus on the "analysis ... of social systems and social structures" have been classified by Abercrombie et al. (1988 p.141) as macro-sociological, whereas those which focus on the analysis of "face-to-face social encounters in everyday life and ... interpersonal behaviour in small groups" are classified as micro-sociological. (Abercrombie et al. 1988 p.155) For a study such as this, which involves consideration of both global and local, societal and individual issues, and in which it is sometimes difficult to distinguish between the structural and interpretive aspects of particular issues, social scientific theories which do not to address the structure and agency issues together but deal with them separately do not provide an appropriate framework of reference.

The Natural Sciences - Social Sciences 'Problem'

Given the focus of this study on human social behaviour which relates specifically to the physical environment, another (related) 'problem' - the distinction which is often made or assumed between the social sciences on the one hand and the 'natural' sciences on the other - is also relevant.

Dickens (1992 p.2) writes:

> the social and the natural sciences have all made great strides in their own field of specialism and each now has its own well-developed discourse. But the problem is that they are talking past each other. We have a dichotomous understanding, one based on science, the other on social theory. So, while social theory can certainly continue to make major contributions, the danger is that it will do so within its comparatively watertight disciplinary compartments. Much the same could be said of the sciences, such as physics, chemistry and biology.

In order to deal with this dichotomy, Dickens suggests that there needs to be a new approach based on a breaking down of "compartmentalised divisions of intellectual labour". (p.3) He suggests that such an approach would be based on social scientists and natural scientists sharing common working methods and perceptions:

> They would share common ways of, for example, understanding organisms (including the human organism) and their relationships with natural-cum-social environments. (Dickens p.3)

The need for the integration of social and natural sciences in the analysis of environmental issues is supported by Martell (1994). According to Martell (p.7), far from being determined largely by the physical environment, human behaviour towards the environment is "driven by economic and social developments and practices". Martell goes on to say:

> structures and processes that are central to the expertise of social scientists are as important to environmental problems as those that are of interest to natural scientists. (p.7)

This view is supported by Yearley (1991) who states:

> social science is important to our appreciation of the green case precisely because there are major social, political and economic aspects to current environmental issues. Although most environmental problems are problems of the natural world and accordingly demand expertise in the natural sciences, this demand is by no means exclusive. In the examples we have studied, it has been clear that social conditions have contributed to bringing about ecological problems and that social change is necessary for their solution. (p.184)

Pepper (1984) demonstrates some of the differences between physical scientists' and social scientists' understandings of the human/nature relationship. He highlights, for example, the tendency of the physical sciences to adopt a position of 'environmental determinism':

> The environment - usually defined in terms of physical factors like (especially) climate, soils, topography - is believed to *influence to the extent of substantially controlling* aspects of human behaviour (individual and group), economic activity and social organisation, and even physiological characteristics. (pp.34-35)

As a contrast to this 'determinist' position, Pepper (p.35) also outlines the 'existentialist' position which "emphasises human personality and free will". He goes on to describe the sociological theory of 'phenomenology', an extension of philosophical existentialism founded by Husserl, which:

> emphasised the importance of human *intentionality* towards the natural world. If we wish to understand the latter, we can do so only through

studying man's intentions towards it and his *consciousness* of it, rather than by trying to study it as some kind of external set of mechanical objects. (Pepper 1984 p.35)

Within this debate about the nature and origins of environmental problems, Martell (pp.7-8) also highlights a further dichotomy confronting the analysis and resolution of such problems: the division between "technocratic environmentalists who see environmental problems as resolvable by the 'technical fix' within existing economic and social practices ... (and) ecologists who see such problems as embedded in economic and social structures and practices and resolvable only by changes at that level".

The Failure of Sociological Theories to Address these Problems

In attempting to understand environmental issues such as the 'greening' of manufacturing industry, through the application of social theory, sociologists are faced with multiple dualisms or dichotomies: the dichotomies between structure and agency, between the natural sciences and the social sciences in their views of human beings' relationship to nature, between environmentalist and ecologist approaches to solving environmental problems, and between the different schools of thought within sociology itself.

Despite the need and rationale (outlined above) for sociological analysis to be applied to environmental problems, there is evidence that this has occurred only to a limited degree. Martell (p.9) draws attention to the finding of Dunlap and Catton (1993) that "not one article on environmental problems ... was published in either of the two main American sociology journals between 1970 and 1990".

According to Dickens, who draws on the arguments put forward by Catton and Dunlap, this failure to develop an interdisciplinary approach to environmental problems is (at least in part) due to the traditional divisions between disciplines. He states:

sociology developed in an era 'when humans seemed exempt from ecological constraints'. Now, as changing ecological conditions are threatening human societies, the time is right ... to reassess sociological theory as it has come down to us since the nineteenth century. ... the disciplinary traditions carved out in the nineteenth century (one for sociology, others for biology and ecology) are not only militating against a solution to ecological problems, they are actually impeding an understanding of their social importance. (Dickens 1992 p.xi)

This 'problem' has led Catton and Dunlap to call for "a new ecological paradigm for a post exuberant sociology". (Dunlap & Catton 1980 pp.15-47)

This plea for a more interdisciplinary approach to environmental problems is supported by Dickens (p.1) who asserts "that social theory is directly applicable and useful to understanding green issues" and also by Yearley (1992 p.184) who says "social science can make a significant contribution to understanding the green case".

Dickens says:

There can be little doubt that the causes of contemporary ecological and environmental problems are largely associated with social relations, social pressures and political institutions. (p.1)

However, as Dickens goes on to point out (p.2), the lack of integration between the social and natural sciences has often meant that social theory has not been effectively used to understand environmental issues.

The Rationale for Selecting Giddens' Structuration Theory as the Framework for this Study

In the light of the preceding discussion, and the need for a framework of social theory for this study which takes account of both the structure and agency issues and which provides a workable basis for considering the relationships between the social and the natural environments, both the structuralist/functionalist and the phenomenological perspectives can be ruled out. Marxian social theory also appears inappropriate in view of what Dickens (p.193) describes as its "tacit anthropocentrism" and the tendency in the 1970s for it to adopt structuralist overtones.

It seems, therefore, as Dickens suggests "that despite increasing concern with environmental and ecological issues, social theory has still not adequately responded to Catton and Dunlap's challenge". (Dickens 1992 p.xiii)

However, Dickens highlights the work of Giddens as offering an opportunity for developing such a paradigm. As noted above, Giddens' structuration theory does integrate structure and agency issues to some extent. And although Giddens does not attempt "to combine the biological and social sciences" (Dickens p.149), his emphasis on 'time-space distanciation' and on the locational embedding of social life has relevance for understanding of both environmental and social systems. (Dickens p.151)

Structuration Theory

In order to overcome the perceived inadequacies of existing social theories (a number of which are outlined above), Anthony Giddens has developed an approach to social analysis known as 'structuration theory'.

In contrast to macro theories such as structural functionalism and micro theories such as phenomenology, which treat 'structure' and 'action' as separate and distinct concepts, Giddens' theory of structuration asserts that social structure and social action are two aspects of the one phenomenon.

Giddens states:

> To study the structuration of a social system is to study the ways in which that system, via the application of generative rules and resources, ... is produced and reproduced in interaction. (Giddens 1979 p.66)

'Structuration', according to Giddens, is "the structuring of social relations across time and space, in virtue of the duality of structure". (1984 p.376)

Abercrombie et al. (1988 p.245) describe structuration as a "concept ... which expresses the mutual dependency rather than opposition of human agency and social structure".

This interdependence of structure and action (agency) which forms the basis of structuration theory is perhaps best summed up by the following quote from Giddens:

> The constitution of agents and structures are not two independently given sets of phenomena, a dualism, but represent a duality. According to the notion of the duality of structure, the structural properties of social systems are both medium and outcome of the practices they recursively organise. (Giddens 1984 p.25)

The relationship between structure and action is rethought by Giddens so that they are not seen as "counteracting elements of a dualism ... (but) as the complementary terms of a duality". (Thompson 1989 p.58) Explaining Giddens' theory of the "'recursive character' of social life", Thompson states (p.58):

> Every act of production is at the same time an act of reproduction: the structures that render an action possible are, in the performance of that action, reproduced.

Giddens uses the example of language to explain this concept of the 'duality of structure', which (along with the concepts of 'structure' and 'system') forms "the core of structuration theory". (Giddens 1984 p.16)

> When I utter a sentence, or make sense of an utterance of somebody else, I draw on an 'absent corpus' of syntactic and semantic rules in order to do so. ... these structural features of the language are the medium whereby I generate an utterance. ... in producing a syntactically correct utterance I simultaneously contribute to the reproduction of the language as a whole. (Giddens 1982, cited in Cassell 1993 p.13)

In Giddens' view, it is only by following the commonly agreed rules of language that communication occurs. In this sense the 'structure' of language is the medium through which humans are empowered or enabled to communicate. At the same time, by using language in accordance with the established rules, humans perpetuate the shared understanding of the rules which govern language. The rules of language, therefore, are both the process and the product of language, hence Giddens' use of the concept of the 'duality of structure'.

Structures, according to Giddens, should be seen not as determinants of human behaviour but rather as factors which both enable and constrain human behaviour. This understanding of social structures is an important feature of structuration theory which distinguishes it from structural-functionalist theories. Giddens (1984 p.xxi) highlights the centrality of this concept to the whole theory of structuration, saying:

> This book, indeed, might be accurately described as an extended reflection upon a celebrated and oft-quoted phrase to be found in Marx ... that 'Men ... make history, but not in circumstances of their own choosing'.

In Giddens' view, 'structures' are not objective realities which are external to human beings, but instead consist of 'rules' and 'resources' which are the structuring properties through which the reproduction of social systems occurs. So, using the example of language, the rules of the English language which govern conversations both constrain the speaker (ie. act as 'rules') and facilitate or empower communication (ie. act as 'resources'). Because 'rules' are not objective realities but are dependent for their perpetuation on their application by members of society, they may be modified in the process of interaction. Thus, according to Giddens, "all rules are inherently transformational". (1984 p.17)

Giddens identifies two forms of resources: 'allocative resources' and 'authoritative resources'. "Allocative resources refer to capabilities ... generating command over objects, goods or material phenomena". (1984 p.33) These include such items as land, raw materials, technologies, means of production and outputs of production. "Authoritative resources refer to types of transformative capacity generating command over persons or actors". (1984 p.33) Such resources relate to the ability of some individuals to dominate others. Just as rules can be reproduced or changed by human actors, so also resources are created, maintained and changed through human actions.

The third key concept of structuration theory is that of social 'systems'. In structuration theory, 'social systems' are not structures in themselves but exhibit structural properties (ie. rules and resources). Social systems can be described as patterns of social relations existing over time and space.

In Giddens' view, 'time' and space' should not simply be treated as contexts or environments in which social behaviour takes place, but as integral to that behaviour. Giddens defines 'time-space distanciation' as "the stretching of social systems across time-space, on the basis of mechanisms of social and system integration". (1984 p.377) In Giddens' view, "the greater the time-space distanciation of social systems - the more their institutions bite into time and space - the more resistant they are to manipulation or change by any individual agent". (1984 p.171)

The reproduction of social systems occurs through the action of individual 'actors' or 'agents', and is based on shared knowledge and the need for 'ontological security' which Giddens defines as "confidence or trust that the natural and social worlds are as they appear to be". (1984 p.375)

The transformation of social systems, on the other hand, occurs as a result of what Giddens (1984) describes as 'reflexive monitoring of actions'. Through this process, humans monitor their own and others' conduct to determine whether the outcomes which were intended to be achieved through the conduct have, in fact been achieved. Where objectives are not being achieved, new patterns of behaviour may be initiated.

In considering the action (or 'agency') taken by human beings, Giddens distinguishes 'action' or 'agency' from 'intention', since he believes that actions often have unintended consequences. 'Intentional' behaviour is defined by Giddens as "an act which its perpetrator knows, or believes, will have a particular quality or outcome and where such knowledge is utilised by the author of the act to achieve this quality or outcome". (1984 p.10) He states:

> The *durée* (defined as 'a continuous flow of conduct') of day-to-day life occurs as a flow of intentional action. However, acts have unintended consequences .... (which) may systematically feed back to be the unacknowledged conditions of further acts. Thus one of the regular consequences of my speaking or writing English in a correct way is to contribute to the reproduction of the English language as a whole. My speaking English correctly is intentional; the contribution I make to the reproduction of the language is not. (1984 p.8)

Giddens also considers motivations for action, which he defines as "the wants which prompt (action)". (1984 p.6) According to Giddens, individuals are not always aware of their motivations for action. He states:

> While competent actors can nearly always report discursively about their intentions in, and reasons for, acting as they do, they cannot necessarily do so of their motives. Unconscious motivation is a significant feature of human conduct .... (1984 p.6)

Similarly, Giddens distinguishes between "discursive and practical consciousness". (1984 p.7) He defines discursive consciousness as "what actors are able to say, or to give verbal expression to, about social conditions, including especially the conditions of their own action" (p.374), whereas practical consciousness is defined as "what actors know (believe) about social conditions, including especially the conditions of their own action, but cannot express discursively". (p.375)

The Application of Structuration Theory to Environmental Sociology

Based on the literature review and the outline of Giddens' theory of structuration, there appear to be a number of aspects of this theory which have relevance to environmental sociology in general (the examination of human behaviour in relation to the natural world) and to this study in particular.

There have been obvious and significant changes in the 'social systems' (ie. patterns of social relations existing over time and space) associated with environmental behaviour over recent years. An analysis of the 'structuration' of those systems (ie. the ways in which those systems are produced, reproduced and modified through interaction) would offer understandings of that behaviour, and could identify opportunities and mechanisms for future change.

Giddens' concept of the 'duality of structure' has particular relevance for environmental sociology. According to this concept, structuring properties of social systems may be seen as both the medium and outcome of social behaviour. A number of structuring properties relating to environmental behaviour can be identified, such as regulatory frameworks and economic instruments. These can be examined to identify their inherent dualities, and to consider the opportunities which such structures offer for reproduction and transformation of patterns of environmental behaviour in the future.

On another level, also, 'duality of structure' may be seen to be relevant to a study such as this. In structuration theory, structures are seen as factors which both constrain and facilitate human behaviour. The physical environment within which such interaction takes place provides a structure - rules and resources - which limits or constrains the behavioural choices which can be made by humans. For example, Miller & Armstrong (1982) cite some of the basic 'rules' or 'laws' of nature which constrain human behaviour:

> the *law of conservation of energy*, also known as the *first law of thermodynamics*, (which states that) energy is neither created nor destroyed in any ordinary physical or chemical process, but merely changed from one form to another; (p. 26)

and:

the *law of conservation of matter:* (which states that) in any ordinary physical or chemical change, matter is neither created nor destroyed but only transformed from one form to another. (p. 24)

At the same time, there are social structures ('rules' and 'resources') which also impact on human interaction with the physical environment. For example, physical structures may be (and frequently are) changed by human intervention. Ironbridge (UK), known as the birthplace of the Industrial Revolution, might also be called 'the birthplace of the Greenhouse effect'. Resource depletion and pollution, which result from human intervention in the environment, change the environment itself: acid rain results in forest die-back; pollution of rivers leaves them virtually lifeless; deforestation turns productive land into desert. On the other hand, technology may be used to overcome environmental degradation - a case of human intervention transforming the physical structure in a positive way. Structuration theory offers a way of looking at human environmental behaviour which takes into account both the social and physical structures which constrain and facilitate such behaviour.

Dickens (pp.145-146) highlights another important aspect of Giddens' structuration theory which has relevance for environmental sociology - "his emphasis on time and space". Dickens says:

People's interactions and the remaking of social structures do not occur on the head of a pin. They are all embedded in contexts or 'locales'. At the same time, however, social systems are increasingly stretched over time and space. International markets, telecommunications and multinational corporations are all part of a process whereby society is taking on an increasingly globalised character. (p.146)

This 'time-space distanciation' is similar in some ways to the Marxian concept of alienation. Dickens (p.152) points to "the spatial and temporal separation of people from nature" which have resulted from the development of modern industrial societies. The impacts of extracting inputs from the environment (in terms of resources) and imposing outputs on the environment (in terms of pollution) are often separated from individuals and communities on time and space dimensions. As a result, impacts on local environments often originate in different times and places. Communities thus lack understanding and control over such impacts which, Giddens asserts, has a profound effect on their 'ontological security' - "their sense of 'being' or 'being in the world'". (Dickens p.147) In the context of this study, which involves companies which are both 'local' and 'multinational', as well as companies with a long history and those which are relatively new, it is important to have a theoretical framework which provides for an analysis on the basis of 'time-space distanciation'.

Further aspects of Giddens' structuration theory which have relevance for this study (given its focus on the motivations for the 'greening' of industry) include his reflections on intentionality and unintended consequences, on conscious and unconscious motivations, and on discursive and practical consciousness.

5 Methodological Approach

Introduction

The choice made by sociologists of what they will study and how they will study it depends on the assumptions underlying their research. Such assumptions relate to sociologists' beliefs about the inherent nature of social life and of human behaviour. For example, the type of issues considered will include: the nature of reality and the processes for acquiring knowledge about it; whether social life is seen as determined by external or internal forces; and the extent of rationality given to human behaviour.

One approach to sociological research is founded on the principle of 'positivism': the view that "in spite of the differences in subject matter of the various scientific disciplines, both natural and social, the same method or logic of explanation can be used". (Blaikie 1993 p.13)

Within sociology, there is a tendency for positivist approaches to be linked with "social structural explanations as distinct from those which refer to human intentions and motives". (Abercrombie et al. 1988 p.190)

As Jones (1985 p.80) explains:

> Structural theorists, who believe social behaviour to be the product of external social forces, are most likely to argue for the use of scientific methods to acquire knowledge of these structural forces.

Such methods are known in sociology as 'positivist methods', and the data produced is primarily quantitative. Giddens (1984 p.329) concurs, saying:

> A fondness for quantitative methods has, of course, long been a trait of those attracted to objectivism and structural sociology. According to this type of standpoint, analysing conditions of social life that stretch well beyond any immediate contexts of interaction is the prime objective of social science, and grasping the 'hardened' nature of the institutional

components of social life can best be accomplished through classification, measurement and statistical methods.

Another approach to sociological research is based on 'hermeneutics' - "the theory and method of interpreting meaningful human action". (Abercrombie et al. 1988 p.112) Those who follow this approach are often known as 'interpretive' or 'phenomenological' sociologists.

Phenomenological sociologists take the view that the analysis and description of social life should be based on the understandings and interpretations of the people involved, rather than on the basis of any assumptions concerning the impact of external social structures.

Jones (1985 p.80), comparing structural theorists with those who adopt a more interpretive approach, states:

> Interpretive theorists, in contrast, see things rather differently. For them, social behaviour is the outcome of people's abilities to interpret the world around them.   Consequently, they believe that science is a wholly inappropriate way of acquiring understanding of social life.

The methods used by interpretive theorists are described as 'anti-positivist' or 'interpretivist', and the data generated is qualitative.

Giddens' theory of structuration attempts to bridge the gap between structural theory and phenomenology.   In doing so, it poses some questions concerning its 'domain assumptions' and therefore about appropriate methodologies.   Blaikie (1993 p.90) points out that whilst Giddens rejects positivism and argues in favour of explanation and understanding, he nevertheless "has recognised, what Interpretivists have neglected, that ... actions occur within a framework of unacknowledged conditions and unintended consequences".   However, the fact that Giddens believes that structures may be changed by human actions taken after reflexive monitoring of the achievement of objectives indicates a leaning towards the interpretive end of the scale.   This is confirmed by Giddens' own statement that:

> Social life cannot even be accurately described by a sociological observer, let alone causally elucidated, if that observer does not master the array of concepts employed (discursively or non-discursively) by those involved. (Giddens 1987, cited in Cassell 1993 p.149)

Giddens asserts that social research occurs at four related levels:

1 Hermeneutic elucidation of frames of meaning.
2 Investigation of context and form of practical consciousness.
3 Identification of bounds of knowledgeability.
4 Specification of institutional orders. (Giddens 1984 pp.327-330)

According to Giddens (1984 pp.327-330), the first two levels of research are commonly associated with qualitative methods, whereas levels 3 and 4 are more commonly linked with quantitative methods. He says:

> Those who favour quantitative methods as the main basis of what makes social science 'science' are prone to emphasise the primacy of so-called macrosociological analysis. Those who advocate qualitative methods as the foundation of empirical research in the social sciences, on the other hand, emphasise (1) and (2) in order to point up the necessarily situated and meaningful character of social interaction. ... It is not difficult to see in the conflict between these positions a methodological residue of the dualism of structure and action, and showing such a dualism to be spurious will allow us to tease out further some of the empirical implications of the duality of structure. (pp. 329-330)

Giddens (1984 p.327-328) points out that (although) "the methodological 'insertion' of the research investigator into whatever material is the object of study can be made at any of the four levels indicated above (nevertheless) all social research presumes a hermeneutic moment". Therefore, in keeping with this inclusion of interpretive 'domain assumptions' in Giddens' theory of structuration, the methodological approach used for this study is interpretivist or anti-positivist and the research strategy is primarily abductive.

According to Blaikie (1993 p.176) "abduction is the process used to produce social scientific accounts of social life by drawing on the concepts and meanings used by social actors, and the activities in which they engage". As a research strategy, abduction has multiple layers, depicted by Blaikie (1993 p.177) as follows (Figure 5.1):

> *Everyday concepts and meanings*
> provide the basis for
> *Social action/interaction*
> about which
> *Social actors can give accounts*
> from which
> *Social scientific descriptions can be made*
> from which   OR   and understood in terms of
> *Social theories can be generated*   *Social theories or perspectives*

Figure 5.1:   **Multiple Layers of Abductive Research**
Source: Blaikie, 1993

In Blaikie's view, such a strategy is entirely appropriate to the type of study reported in this book. He states:

> In those branches of Interpretivism that are concerned to go beyond description to explanation and prediction, it is argued that Abduction is the appropriate research strategy. Such a strategy involves constructing theory which is derived from social actors' language, meanings and theories, or is grounded in everyday activities. Such research begins by describing these activities and meanings and then deriving from them categories and concepts that can form the basis of an understanding or an explanation of the problem at hand. (1993 p.163)

Research Methods

Key Research Method

The key method adopted for this research is the case study.

A case study is described by Abercrombie et al. (1988 p.28) as "the detailed examination of a single example of a class of phenomena". Abercrombie et al. go on to say: "Many case-study investigations in fact use more than a single case, in order to get some idea of the range of variability in the population under consideration". Such is the case for this research.

Table 5.1, extracted from Yin (1989 p.17) compares a range of research strategies in terms of their relevance for particular situations.

According to Yin (1989 p.19), "the case study is preferred in examining contemporary events, but when the relevant behaviours cannot be manipulated". Hence the relevance of the case study method for this research.

Table 5.1: Relevant Situations for Different Research Strategies

Strategy	Form of Research Question	Requires Control over Behavioural Events?	Focuses on Contemporary Events?
Experiment	How, Why	Yes	Yes
Survey	Who, What *, Where, How Many, How Much	No	Yes
Archival analysis (eg. economic study)	Who, What *, Where, How Many, How Much	No	Yes/No
History	How, Why	No	No
Case Study	How, Why	No	Yes

* "What" questions, when asked as part of an exploratory study, pertain to all five strategies.

Overall Research Design

The research design for this study has included both primary and secondary data collection methods, and has comprised three key elements: a literature review; interviews with key informants; and (as noted above) case study interviews. Specific tasks have included:

- identification, acquisition and review of relevant literature;
- collection of relevant background information through interviews (both telephone and face-to-face) with relevant 'experts' in Australia and overseas;
- selection of companies for detailed study;
- establishment of contact with appropriate key informants in companies;
- conduct of face-to-face interviews with key informants;

- collation of data from key informant interviews and preparation of 'case study notes';
- distribution of case study notes to companies for perusal and comment;
- revision of case study notes (as necessary) in response to feedback;
- follow-up contact with key informants in companies by letter or telephone (at least six months after initial interviews) to clarify any uncertainties relating to information obtained through initial interviews, to explore any new issues which have arisen and to gain a longitudinal perspective on companies in the study;
- revision of case study notes as necessary in response to information gained through follow-up;
- analysis of case study data; and
- preparation of thesis.

It should be noted that both the literature review and the collection of relevant background information continued throughout the study.

Description of the Research Population

As indicated above, no adequate system has yet been devised for classifying companies, products or production processes as 'environmentally preferred'.   The development of such a classification system is beyond the scope of a study such as this, and to wait for such a development would have delayed the commencement of this research for some years, thereby undermining the relevance of this research. However, progress in this area will continue to be monitored, and adjustments will be made as necessary to the data included as part of the study.

The population for this study has been drawn from three sources:

- the list of eighteen companies which had had their environmental claims verified under the 'Environmental Choice Australia' program (as at July 16, 1992);
- the 400 small businesses which were listed in the 1992 Green Directory published by the Victorian Department of Small Business; and
- the list of green products and their manufacturers being developed by the Centre for Design, RMIT.

Whilst it is acknowledged that none of these listings provides any guarantee that the companies, products or processes included will fulfil any future criteria which may be used to define 'environmentally preferred', in the absence of any comprehensive classification system these listings provided the best available alternative.

From these listings, 249 companies which were not involved in manufacturing were eliminated, leaving a population of more than 169 companies.

Sampling Method

In order to ensure that a range of companies, products and processes were included in the sample, each of the companies in the population was classified according to a number of criteria:

- whether the products manufactured are 'environmentally corrective', 'environmentally ameliorative', or 'environmentally benign'; and
- whether the products manufactured are primarily for the industrial, commercial, agricultural or domestic consumer markets.

It is important to acknowledge that, despite the efforts to ensure that a range of products, processes and companies were included in the study, (including environmentally corrective, ameliorative and benign products, and those aimed at the commercial, industrial, agricultural and domestic markets), the sampling method used for this study was not designed to be representative. As Yin (1989 p.21) points out:

> case studies, like experiments, are generalisable to theoretical propositions and not to populations or universes. In this sense, the case study, like the experiment, does not represent a 'sample', and the investigator's goal is to expand and generalise theories (analytic generalisation) and not to enumerate frequencies (statistical generalisation).

Accordingly, the selection of companies for study (within the parameters outlined above) has been made largely on an opportunistic basis - that is, companies have been selected because of their accessibility to the researcher and their willingness to participate.

In keeping with the abductive strategy described in the 'grounded theory' approach put forward by Glaser and Strauss (stated by Blaikie 1993 p.193 to provide "the most explicit exposition available of a genuine Abductive research strategy"), the size of the sample was not determined at the beginning of the study. Instead the concept of "theoretical saturation" was used.

> Saturation means that no additional data are being found whereby the sociologist can develop properties of the category. ....When one category is saturated, nothing remains but to go to new groups for data on other categories, and attempt to saturate these new categories also.   When saturation occurs, the analyst will usually find that some gap in his (sic) theory, especially in his major categories, is almost, if not completely filled. (Glaser and Strauss 1968 p.61)

In all, thirty companies were included in the study.

Data Collection

The primary method of data collection was the focused interview. Following initial telephone contact to ascertain the companies' willingness to participate in the study, and to arrange a date and time for an interview, each company was sent a letter of confirmation of the arrangements. This letter also contained an outline of the research topic and some broad questions which would be explored through the interview. These included:

- In your opinion, who or what influenced the company to produce green products?
- What was the process by which your company came to be involved in producing such a product/s?
- How successful do you consider the company to be/have been?
- To what extent do you perceive the company's success to be related to the 'greenness' of its product/s?
- In your opinion, what factors (both internal and external) have assisted the company?
- In your opinion, what factors (both internal and external) have hindered the company?

- What policy initiatives do you believe should be taken by government/s to promote development of green industry in Australia?
- What conditions outside the direct control of government/s do you believe are needed to encourage such development?

Initial interviews lasted, on average, about an hour, and most were recorded on audio tape as well as in written note form. Case study notes were sent to companies for review and comment, and adjustments were made where necessary.

Follow-up was undertaken (either by letter or by letter combined with telephone or personal interview) approximately 6 - 12 months after the initial interviews. This follow-up served a number of purposes: to clarify any uncertainties relating to the information obtained in the initial interviews; to explore any new issues which had come to light during the course of the study; and to gain a longitudinal perspective on the companies included in the sample. For several companies in the sample, this longitudinal perspective uncovered significant changes in the companies' situation: one had been placed in receivership; another had been taken over by its equity partners.

Data Analysis

Analysis of Case Study Data

In keeping with the qualitative nature of the data, initial analysis of the data was descriptive. The data obtained from each company have been classified according to a number of key themes. Each case study has been written up in a similar format for ease of comparison, and four of these are included in this book. In writing the case study notes, Giddens' observation that "the social scientist is a communicator, introducing frames of meaning associated with certain contexts of social life to those in others" (Giddens 1984 p.285) was taken into account. Care has therefore been taken to avoid (wherever possible) "thick description". (Giddens 1984 p.285)

Subsequently, a more detailed analysis of the data was undertaken, considering it from the perspective of the motivational factors (see Chapters 6 and 7), the factors which assisted companies (see Chapter 8), the factors which hindered companies (see Chapter 9), and the conditions which would be required for future expansion of the greening of industry (see Chapter 11). Matrices depicting the spread of opinions across the whole sample were developed and are included in the relevant chapters.

Under each of the broad headings, key themes were identified and discussed in detail, including linkages with the literature and the theoretical framework.

Development of a Typology

In order that the data generated through this study may be built upon and tested by other researchers, it is important to move from first-order constructs (the understandings of the social actors studied) to second-order constructs (typifications based on social science understandings of the relevant data).

The concepts of first-order and second-order constructs were generated by Schütz (1963). He stated:

> The thought objects constructed by the social scientist, in order to grasp this social reality, have to be founded upon the thought objects constructed by the common-sense thinking of men [sic], living their daily life within their social world. Thus, the constructs of the social sciences are, so to speak, constructs of the second degree, that is, constructs of the constructs made by the actors on the social scene, whose behaviour the social scientist has to observe and to explain. (p.242)

As Blaikie (1993 p.180) notes:

> The move from first-order to second-order constructs requires the social scientist to select from the activities and meanings of everyday life those considered to be relevant to the purpose at hand and to construct models of the social world - typical social actors with typical motives and typical courses of action in typical situations.

This process is known as the development of "ideal types".

> Ideal types are ... hypothetical constructions, formed from real phenomena, which have an explanatory value. 'Ideal' signifies 'pure' or 'abstract' rather than normatively desirable. (Abercrombie et al. 1988 p.117)

Typologies (sets of 'ideal types') are constructed by the social scientist selecting "from the activities and meanings of everyday life those considered to be relevant to the purpose at hand and to construct models of the social world - typical social actors with typical motives and typical courses of action in typical situations". (Blaikie 1993 p.180)

Blau and Scott (1963) distinguished between typologies based on single descriptive characteristics of organisations, such as size, criteria for membership, the functions they perform for society, and so on, and typologies based on more analytical characterisations. Examples of this latter group include Parsons' 'functional' typology of organisations based on which fundamental need of society they are designed to meet, Thompson and Tuden's typology based on the decision making processes in organisations, and the *cui bono* typology of organisations developed by Blau and Scott based on 'who benefits' from the operations of the organisation. (Blau and Scott 1963 pp.42-45)

Etzioni's (1961) 'compliance' typology - one of the more complex typologies, based on analytical classifications - was developed by identifying the types of power within organisations and the types of involvement in organisations, then cross-tabulating the two characteristics to identify the range of types of organisations. 'Power' is defined by Etzioni as "an actor's ability to induce or influence another actor to carry out his directives or any other norms he supports". (Etzioni 1970 p.60) 'Involvement' is defined as "the cathectic-evaluative orientation of an actor to an object, characterised in terms of intensity and direction". (Etzioni 1970 p.64) Cross-classification of the two sets of characteristics resulted in the identification of nine possible types of organisations, three of which included the majority of cases. These cross-classifications formed the basis of the organisational typology.

Typologies are generally required to demonstrate four key features:

- Categories which are mutually exclusive.
- Categories which are based on comprehensive data.
- Categories which are discrete.
- A recognisable theoretical basis.

Blaikie (1993 p.181) points out that, according to Schütz's model, "if social actors cannot identify with the types which have been constructed to represent their actions or situations, then the researcher has either got it wrong or has strayed too far from the concepts of everyday life".

Chapter Ten proposes a tentative typology of companies based on the data from this study. It was developed by classifying the companies in the sample according to the primary motivational factors influencing their 'greening' (as nominated by the key informants from each case study company). It remains tentative, as it is based on information obtained from a small sample (thirty companies) and therefore does not fulfil criterion two (above). However, it offers a starting point for the future development of a more comprehensive typology.

6 Why Companies Go 'Green' - What the Literature Says

Theories of Motivation

The complexity of the whole issue of motivations, and of accurately identifying the reasons for behaviour is noted by Kemp (1990). He quotes Mills (1940 p.904) as saying: "The differing reasons men give for their actions are not themselves without reasons". Kemp goes on to say:

> The need is therefore to look beyond the superficial explanations given and elucidated for social and political behaviour, and to determine the structural, institutional, and contextual factors which contribute to the employment of particular forms of reasoning. (1990 p.1247)

In emphasising the context-specific nature of motivations, Kemp cites Mannheim (1940 p.249) who stated: "both motives and actions very often originate not from within but from the situation in which individuals find themselves".

Most of the literature on motivations is based on psychological theories. As Shamir (1991) notes, the current plethora of explanations of industrial organisational behaviour from a motivational perspective are confusing and inadequate. In Shamir's view, these theories offer inadequate explanations of motivation within organisations for several reasons:

- their focus on individual rather than collective factors;
- their inapplicability in situations not "characterised by clear goals, availability of rewards and strong rewards-performance relationship"; (p.407)
- their concern with discrete acts rather than with "the repetition or continuation of such acts ... or ... broader patterns of behaviour *containing* many different acts performed over time and space"; (p.408)

59

- their failure to acknowledge that although a task may lack any "psychologically gratifying properties" or any "rewards", it may motivate the individual because of its meaning for her/him, "for instance in terms of the affirmation of his or her identity and collective affiliations"; (p.409) and
- their interpretation of 'values' as "preferences" rather than as "conceptions of the desirable". (p.410)

Given these constraints, such theoretical explanations appear to have limited relevance to the discussion of corporate motivations for environmentalism.

However, Shamir (pp.411-414) goes on to outline a new theory of work motivation based on the notion of self-concept. The theory is based on five underlying assumptions:

- that human beings act in ways which express their self-concept, not just in goal-oriented ways;
- that maintenance and enhancement of self-esteem and self-worth are important motivators;
- that retention and increase of internal consistency (between different aspects of the self-concept, in terms of continuity over time and between self-concept and behaviour) is important to people;
- that self-concepts include identities (as well as values); and
- that behaviour which is based on self-concept "is not always related to clear expectations or to immediate and specific goals". (p.413)

In emphasising the importance of self-concept in directing human behaviour, Shamir posits the view that self-expression rather than opportunism is the "core tendency of human behaviour". (p.411) He goes on to say:

Making this assumption enables us to account for behaviours that are not instrumental for the individual and do not even contribute to the individual's satisfaction. (1991 p.411)

The differences between self-esteem ("based on a sense of competence, power or achievement") and self-worth ("based on a sense of virtue and moral worth") are also highlighted by Shamir (p.412), who notes that individuals evaluate their behaviour against these two types of standards. He quotes Bandura as saying:

> Much of (people's) behaviour is motivated and regulated by internal
> standards and self-evaluative reactions to their own actions. (Bandura 1986
> p.2, cited in Shamir p.412)

Internal consistency is also important in people's work motivation,
according to Shamir. He states:

> People derive a sense of 'meaning' from a sense of unity of their self-
> concept, from continuity between the past, the present and the projected
> future (McHugh 1968) and from the correspondence between their
> behaviour and self-concept. (p.412)

The notion that self-concepts include identities as well as values - the
third of Shamir's assumptions - is important in any understanding of work
motivation, as 'workers' have multiple identities such as 'parent',
'bushwalker', 'Christian', 'Democrat' and so on. Shamir notes that,
according to Stryker's identity theory (Stryker 1980), these multiple
identities:

> are organised in the self-concept according to a hierarchy of salience.
> Identity salience is defined as the importance of an identity for defining
> one's self, relative to other identities held by the individual. ... the higher
> the salience of an identity within the self-concept the greater its
> motivational significance. (Shamir 1991 p.413)

The final element of Shamir's set of assumptions relates to the timing
and tangibility of behaviour outcomes. According to Shamir, behaviour is
often related to visions and aspirations rather than real expectations or
short-term goals. Shamir draws on the work of Markus and Nurius (1986),
using the concept of 'possible selves' which are defined as "individuals'
ideas of what they might become, what they would like to become and
what they are afraid of becoming". (Shamir p.414)
Shamir goes on to say:

> An individual's repertoire of possible selves can be viewed as the cognitive
> and personalised carriers of enduring goals, aspirations, motives, fears and
> threats and of the associated affective states. Thus they provide ... an
> essential link between the self-concept and motivation. (p.414)

Although Shamir's intention was to develop a theory of motivation relevant to work, rather than a theory of motivation relevant to work-related environmentalism, it does appear to have relevance to such behaviour.

To some degree, at least, the conditions suggested by Shamir as appropriate for the application of the theory correspond with the conditions affecting companies which are involved in pro-environmental behaviours. For example, Shamir indicates that the theory applies in circumstances where "external rewards are not clearly related to performance or goal attainment, due to difficulties in performance evaluation, the dearth of external rewards, or cultural and organisational restrictions imposed on the reward distribution system". (p.415) He also notes the applicability of the theory as an "explanation of 'deviant', non-conforming behaviour". (p.415) Both of these criteria apply to some degree to 'green' companies.

Motivational Factors in the 'Greening' of Industry

According to Marsh (1991 p.318), most Australian businesses can be classified as one of the following four broad types in respect of their relationship to the environment:

> Type 1: those who deliberately break the law (eg. by pumping toxic waste into the stormwater or sewerage systems).
> Type 2: those who break the law because of a lack of interest and/or outdated or inadequate systems (eg. inadequate testing equipment may fail to detect high levels of toxins in food).
> Type 3: those who work within the current legislative framework but who argue that social concern is the responsibility of governments.
> Type 4: those who show a strong proactive concern for protecting the environment and are prepared to invest in 'safe' technologies and products.

The focus of this research is on the last group - the group which might be called 'green business'.

A number of motivations for corporate environmentalism have emerged from the literature. Among these are factors such as "increasing public pressures, skyrocketing cleanup costs, rising criminal and civil liabilities, and stringent laws and regulations" (Bhat 1995 p.9). However, these motivations cannot always easily be separated, as Smith (1991) points out. Apart from the motivation of "responsibility for its own sake", identified by Mintzberg (1983), Smith says:

> The current wave of apparent corporate concern for the environment (and there are some who would claim that it is not a real concern but merely a case of good corporate public relations) would seem to lie at the nexus of the remaining driving forces outlined by Mintzberg, namely enlightened self-interest, investment theory and regulation avoidance. (1991 p.192)

Wook Lee and Green (1994) support the view that there are complex interactions of motivational factors behind the 'greening' of industry. They have developed a model which indicates that cleaner production is prompted by a combination of four key types of factors: compliance (in which they include regulations and standards, as well as pressure from non-governmental organisations); new opportunity; competitive advantage; and social responsibility.

What follows is a discussion of a number of individual motivating factors identified through the literature which operate separately or together in encouraging companies to improve their environmental performance.

Awareness/Recognition of Environmental Problems

Leighton (1992 p.27) says:

> The single greatest influence on the greening of corporations has been the recognition that durable poisons, like chlorinated compounds and heavy metals, are accumulating in the biosphere and pose a serious risk to human and planetary health. Out of that recognition has evolved a more environmentally sensitive way of looking at materials and technologies.

As a result, companies have devised new processes which prevent pollution rather than dealing with it after the event.

Elkington (1987) also points to cases where specific evidence of environmental problems has led to reformulation of products to more environmentally benign design. He cites the OPEC oil crisis of 1973-74 as resulting in the development of cars with improved energy efficiency.

However, Elkington cautions that:

One of the key factors influencing leading industrialists to support the drive for sustainable development ... is not easily reproduceable. Often such people get involved because they have seen the damage caused by present development approaches with their own eyes. (1987 p.156)

Environmental awareness is also one of the factors promoting cleaner production identified by Wook Lee and Green (1994) in their category of 'social responsibility' factors.

Winter (1988) indicates that awareness of the existence of environmental problems is, on its own, not enough to motivate the vast majority of people to take action. He points out that:

Although the phenomenon of forest die-back in Germany has become glaringly obvious even to the layman; although ... the pollution of rivers has reached such a pitch that there is practically no life left in them, there are still too few people who are prepared to take action to get the situation improved. (p.17)

To overcome this apathy, German scientists in 1986 drew up an "ecological balance sheet" (Wicke 1986 p.123) which translated the costs of environmental damage into monetary equivalents - language which would assist most people to understand the extent of the problem. (Winter 1988)

The Development of Full-cost Accounting

According to Leighton (1992 p.27), the traditional cost-benefit method of analysis of company operations is being challenged by the need to accommodate the environment. This view is supported by Dr. David Suzuki (an active media environmentalist) who has pointed to the shortcomings of current accounting procedures, and has called for the development of "accounting procedures which explicitly recognise the full costs of all the inputs into the production process for products and the costs associated with their use and disposal". (Marsh 1991 p.320) Leighton (1992 p.27) reports that:

This emerging holistic approach to production and consumption has given us: the environmental audit, cradle-to-grave product design and management, life-cycle analysis and full-cost accounting - all powerful concepts now being tested in major corporations and many governments.

Such an approach - including all the environmental externalities in the cost of products - gives a clearer message to consumers about the actual cost of the products they are using, and provides a greater incentive for consumers to purchase environmentally preferred products. This assists in the development and maintenance of green industries. As Elkington puts it:

> If industry is charged a good deal of money for the privilege of discharging its effluents to the environment, then investment in pollution control equipment and cleaner production technologies will obviously make a great deal more economic sense than if the environment were to be a free commodity. (1987 p.210)

The Effect of Accidents

Environmental accidents and incidents, such as Bhopal, Three Mile Island and Minimata, although predominantly negative in their impact, do have positive impacts in that they confront companies with their negligence or culpability. Leighton points to the lesson learned from the Union Carbide gas leak at Bhopal, India - that companies which are secretive, rather than publicly accountable, bear more culpability in the event of a disaster. Leighton (1992 p.28) quotes the Chairman of Monsanto, Richard Mahoney as saying: "Bhopal galvanised my thinking in terms of reducing risk and communicating with the public".

According to Leighton:

> Public accountability is now being seen as an important means for the chemical business to recover from what Mahoney calls 'being at near-zero in the public mind'. (1992 p.28)

However, the effects of environmental accidents on corporate decision making have spread beyond the petro-chemical industry. Brown (1995) quotes Dr. Hugh Somerville, the head of environment at British Airways:

> It's very difficult for top management to understand all the environmental issues and to understand their exposure. I suspect one of the things that motivates companies is that they see what happens in a Bhopal or an Exxon Valdez and they decide they need to bring a focus on it. (Somerville, cited in Brown 1995)

A flow-on effect of environmental incidents and accidents has been the increase in corporate insurance premiums, and the expansion in the number of exclusions from policies. As Welford (1994 p.8) points out:

> While it is still possible to find insurance cover for pollution which is sudden, accidental and unforeseen, there are very few insurance companies which will cover general pollution risks unless an environmental audit has been carried out.

Another issue related to environmental incidents and accidents is the effect that public perception of the environmental performance of companies has on their share prices (Smith 1991 p.192).

The Influence of Environmentalists

Environmentalists and environmental groups play an important role in changing corporate directions and behaviour, as Leighton (1992 p.28) highlights:

> Practically unthinkable just two or three years ago, it is now acknowledged within environmentally aware companies and governments that well-informed environmentalists bring valuable opinions to the table. In fact, their involvement may well become a necessity.

Elkington (1987 p.60) also highlights the role of environmental groups, saying: "Increasingly ... environmental NGOs (non-government organisations) act as innovators and as demonstrators of alternatives".

Marsh (1991 p.312) supports this view, saying:

> Environmental groups like the Australian Conservation Foundation, Greenpeace and Friends of the Earth have helped translate environmental issues, which are usually discussed at the macro level, into specific courses of action for other people to follow. An example is the *Green Consumer Guide* (Australian Conservation Foundation 1989).

Corporate Environmental Policies

Leighton (1992 p.28) draws attention to the fact that, just as companies develop a mission statement to indicate their corporate financial and strategic objectives, "many are now stating their environmental goals in the same way". This has been encouraged by peak industry groups. Schmidheiny (1992 p.6) notes that

> The International Chamber of Commerce drafted a 'Business Charter for Sustainable Development', which was launched in April 1991 at the Second World Industry Conference on Environmental Management. The Charter, endorsed by 600 firms worldwide by early 1992, encourages companies to 'commit themselves to improving their environmental performance in accordance with these [the Charter's] 16 Principles, to having in place management practices to effect such improvement, to measuring their progress, and to reporting this progress as appropriate internally and externally.

Schmidheiny (1992) goes on to highlight specific national business groups which have adopted similar charters, and which are actively encouraging member companies to adopt environmental policies. The Business Council of Australia is one such organisation which has developed a set of "Principles of Environmental Management" which it says "are intended to assist corporate Australia in the ongoing evolution of better environmental practice". (Business Council of Australia 1992 p.3)

Specific industry groups have also provided a lead in this area, perhaps the most notable being the chemical industry with its "Responsible Care Principles". (Leighton 1992 p.29) Christie, Rolfe and Legard (1995 p.76) also acknowledge the importance of "self-regulation imposed by voluntary associations (such as adherence to the Responsible Care code of the chemical industry)" in motivating companies to adopt cleaner production techniques.

Nash and Ehrenfeld (1996 p.16), referring to voluntary codes of environmental practice such as the Responsible Care program, note that:

> Although these codes differ in numerous ways, they have important features in common. First, each requires companies to adopt environmental management systems and to audit their progress toward the environmental goals they set for themselves. Second, to varying degrees, each calls upon firms to involve outside groups, such as suppliers, customers, and community groups, in their environmental programs.

The influence on small companies of corporate environmental policies within large companies is also recognised by Brown (1995). He says:

several of the most environmentally conscious companies have been using their clout to try and encourage environmental friendliness in their suppliers. The Institute of Business Ethics (IBE) believes that this sort of pressure is valuable. In its recent report, Benefiting Business and the Environment, the IBE says that implementing an environmental program is harder for small companies, particularly where it involves capital outlay: 'If pressure, ideally accompanied by assistance, is coming from larger companies, the outlays will be easier to justify and impetus stronger.'

In the case of the former Australian Chemical Industry Council (ACIC), now part of the Plastics and Chemicals Industry Association (PACIA) adherence to the principles of 'Responsible Care' is a condition of membership of the association.

Both Schmidheiny (1992) and Leighton (1992) point to individual companies which have developed environmental policies. Leighton (1992 p.29) cites the 3M company, which "calls its waste-reduction program 'Pollution Prevention Pays'", and General Motors, which refuses "to accept disposable packaging components from its suppliers". Schmidheiny (1992 p.194) points to the example of Du Pont which in 1989 adopted "a series of goals for improved environmental performance to be achieved over the coming decade".

Senior Management Commitment to Environmental Policies

Leighton (1992) highlights the importance of the commitment of senior management to environmental policies if they are to succeed, saying:

> If environmental policy is to have significant and rapid impact on a big company it must emanate from the top. (p.28)

He goes on to cite several examples: Du Pont's chairman Edgar Woolard Jr. who called himself Du Pont's "chief environmental officer", and the chairman of ICI who, in 1990, "wrote a personal letter to all 134,000 ICI employees worldwide emphasising the company's environmental commitment and informing them that environmental spending would double" (Leighton 1992 p.28).

Another observation made by Leighton is that the trend to high level executive commitment to the environment should continue and even intensify in the coming decade as younger CEOs replace older ones, because, "with a few exceptions, environmental enthusiasm appears to be a symptom of age - the younger you are, the more you care". (p.29)

This view is supported by Ferris (1995), who stresses the age and attitude of executives as important factors in corporate decision making for the environment.

> Today, a lot of companies put a very high premium on the environment, particularly the more cutting-edge high-tech companies. These firms tend to have younger, progressive people in decision making positions: people who generally are more in tune with the environment. (p. 38)

Elkington (1987 p.22) supports this view and points out that this does not just apply to large corporations but to small businesses also. He quotes Anita Roddick, founder and Managing Director of 'The Body Shop', who stated:

> There is something magical about small companies run by people whose thinking was forged in the Sixties. ... You sit down and ask not only how the business should be run, but also what should be done with the profits.

Leighton (1992 p.28) also highlights the importance of the sixties, quoting Mark Plotkin, vice president of the environment group Conservation International:

> Whatever your opinion of the sixties culture, the one sentiment that endures is a respect for nature. It doesn't matter that these people get older and get married, have kids and start moving to the right politically. They care for the environment in a way that many of their parents and grandparents did not.

Another influence affecting the environmental attitudes of corporate decision-makers is their exposure to 'green' attitudes at home. Brown (1995) says:

> many of today's chief executives, after all, are the first generation of bosses to have grown up with environmentalists - their own children - in the home.

Employee Influence on Corporate Environmentalism

Corporate environmentalism will not be achieved through the efforts of senior management alone. Schmidheiny (1992 p.85) states:

> Although individual leaders can make a difference in changing the framework of goals within which a company operates, they cannot transform this into a living reality without a critical mass of other committed individuals.

This view is affirmed by Denton (1994 p.132), who says:

> When CEOs talk of the need to try to control pollution and that it is 'everyone's responsibility' to do so, it is just an empty phrase, a lot of hot air. It means nothing to someone who feels left out of the loop. CEOs can have a 'vision' till they are blue in the face, but people will not get it if they don't understand how all the pieces fit together. By understanding the whole production and delivery process and their place in it, they can make good decisions. Capturing their minds alone is not enough, you must also capture their hearts. If you can give them a stake in the outcome, some personal and financial reason to manage pollution, you can then profit from the experience.

Leighton goes further, pointing not only to the contribution of employees to the achievement of corporate environmental goals, but also to their important contribution in setting those goals. He states:

> Executives run companies but common people make them work. And common people are showing less and less tolerance for environmentally irresponsible companies. People don't leave their convictions with the receptionist when they come to work in the morning. This explains the enthusiasm most employees show for corporate recycling initiatives ... . (1992 p.30)

Pearce (1991) also highlights the role of employees in the environmentalism within businesses. Affirming Shamir's view of the multiple identities of workers, he draws attention to:

> one of the phenomena of the modern-day environmentalism - the green employee. Talking to business in 1989-90 I was impressed by the number of occasions on which I was told that the real pressure to be green was coming not from environmental pressure groups, or even from the green consumer: it was coming from inside business. (1991 p.2)

According to Leighton (1992 p.30), this contribution of individual employees to the growth of corporate environmentalism is being reinforced by the contribution of organised labour.

Organised labour is beginning to state, in an important change of mind, that environmental improvement is an imperative, that jobs should not be the cost of cleanup, and that hazardous working conditions are often related to environmental pollution.

Consumer Demand

Consumer demand is one of two forces identified by Ryan et al. (1990 p.1) as key factors in the greening of the international market.

It is competitiveness in a new green market, where consumer action is expressed both through boycotts of undesirable goods and demand for 'environmentally friendly' goods, that appears to underpin a real change in assessment of the importance of environmental quality for future industry directions.

This factor is also highlighted by Welford (1994 p.8), who states that:

consumers are increasingly willing to switch to products which are in some way more environmentally friendly than their normal purchase. Companies therefore need to demonstrate that their product and their processes cause minimum harm to the environment.

A 1993 survey by MORI in the United Kingdom indicated that "22% of the general public claim to 'Avoid using the services or products of a company which you consider has a poor environmental record'". (Worcester 1994 p.11)

In Australia, a study of approximately 2,000 people undertaken by Blaikie and Ward (1992) found that there is a proportion of people in each age bracket who choose to avoid products because of the perception that they are environmentally damaging, and that this proportion is higher in the 18-24 age bracket than in other age brackets.

An important factor in this move to environmental consumerism is the link, highlighted by Baldassare and Katz (1992 p.604) between "the perception of environmental problems as a threat to personal well-being" and the adoption of environmental practices. Their study found that women, young people, and those at the centre-left of the political spectrum are more likely than other groups to express serious concern about threats to their personal safety as a result of environmental problems. This has implications for industry, as women play a major role in decisions about household purchases, and young people are the future market for industry's products.

According to Elkington (1987), in the case of Dow Chemicals, economics and consumer demand combined to influence the move to more environmentally sound products. Elkington reports that Dow, which was primarily involved in the bulk chemical market (selling large volumes of chemicals to a small number of customers), decided (for economic reasons) to move into the specialist chemicals market (selling small volumes of chemicals to a large number of customers). In making such a move, Dow was faced with the realisation that those small volume customers "may find unacceptable the idea of buying something with Dow on the label ... if (they think) that Dow pollutes the environment with chemicals that give people cancer". (Elkington 1987 p.118)

Changing Regulatory Climate

The other force identified by Ryan et al. is the changing regulatory climate.

> There is ample evidence that many governments see environmental concern as increasing and thus increasing regulation as unavoidable. International protocols for dealing with ozone-depleting chemicals, for example, may still be strongly contested but such contestation is occurring within a regulatory environment - backed by political mandate and scientific evidence - that few would seriously expect to weaken over the coming decade. Significant investment is already being made by industries based on an assessment of the toughening regulatory climate. (1990 p.1)

Leighton concurs with this, saying:

> Environmental regulations are one of the strongest outside influences on corporate behaviour and it's safe to say they will continue to tighten. But market forces will be even stronger and less controllable. Markets are shifting to accommodate the environment and will continue to make companies move on the issues. (1992 p.30)

Christie, Rolfe and Legard (1995 p.76) refer to another regulatory pressure influencing the greening of companies: the "informal regulation imposed by financiers, insurers and major customers who aim to minimise their own exposure to risks of non-compliance with regulations and of poor environmental performance".

However, Smith (1991) notes that there are "spatial imbalances in the severity of controls" which may impact on companies' environmental behaviour. Smith states:

> Although appearing to be behaving in a socially responsible manner in Western countries, companies can also be engaged in the export of waste products and hazardous technologies to the developing world. Such a process ... can be seen as a means of avoiding stricter legislation rather than responding positively to it ... . (p.193)

Nevertheless, together these forces - the 'market pull' of consumer demand, and the 'market push' of increasing regulation - provide a strong motivation for industry to link economic and environmental priorities together.

Cairncross (1991 p.39) concurs, pointing out that the greening of consumer tastes creates a whole new market. "Nothing is more exciting to industry, especially in the sated markets of the rich world. This shift in tastes may be further stimulated by tough regulations set by green governments. These will be an incentive to industry to develop new technologies in order to comply, which companies may then find that they can export when other countries come abreast".

The external influences on the greening of industry are viewed even more broadly by Deloitte Touche Tohmatsu International et al. (1993) . They refer to a "growing array of stakeholders", suggesting that while some companies will voluntarily improve their environmental performance, most will only do so "in response to strong, sustained external pressures". (p.17)

The Influence of Corporate Competition

Corporate competition is, according to Leighton (1992), another important factor in the development of corporate environmentalism. He says:

> Competition dictates that companies must follow rivals who jump out in

front, and there are a growing number of companies that have decided to turn environmental improvement to their competitive advantage. Their competitors will have little choice but to follow. (p.31)

Elkington and Dimmock (1991 p.36) concur, saying: "Inevitably, as corporate environmental performance becomes a competitive issue, so we will see companies behaving in new ways ... ".

This view is supported by Richard Heckert (1992 p.78), from the Du Pont corporation, who says: "Our future depends on our credibility with the general public. If we don't establish that, we don't have a future".

Irvine (1991 p.22) cites several examples of companies which realised that they could gain an economic advantage by adapting to environmental pressures:

two battery makers, Varta and Eveready, got ahead of their competitors by launching mercury-free products in anticipation of Common Market legislation.

Several examples of corporate environmentalism prompted by cost savings and competitive advantage are cited by Denton (1994 p.14). According to Denton:

Eliminating waste, any waste, can be a competitive advantage. Even small improvements can have a dramatic impact on the bottom line.

Denton (p.14) cites three ways in which these cost savings and competitive advantage may occur: through the reduction or elimination of waste (ie. prevention of pollution or waste production); by viewing waste not as "scrap" but as "an unused resource"; and by viewing waste not as an environmental problem but as a business opportunity (eg. establishing a process for dealing with a particular type of waste and selling that expertise/technology to others).

Legal Liability

Under the heading "Reasons for environmentalist business management", Winter (1988 p.22) highlights the serious threat legal liability poses to companies perpetrating environmental damage:

Without environmentalist business management there will be ... a risk of the company being held liable for environmental damage for enormous sums of money, thus jeopardising the future of the company and of all the jobs dependent on it.

Leighton (1992 p.31) cites the examples of the large fine paid by the Exxon company in the wake of the Exxon Valdez incident, and the penalty paid by Union Carbide following the Bhopal gas leak.

Jacobs (1991 p.135) points to the "United States' 'Superfund' legislation (which) makes firms and landlords liable for the condition of their waste disposal sites even after they no longer use or have sold them". According to Jacobs, this legislation has had a significant impact on the standard of corporate environmental care.

According to Denton (1994 p.23), legal liability acts in another way to motivate companies to improve their environmental performance. He cites the case of:

> Werner and Mertz, a medium-sized German chemical company. Consumers had claimed some of its products caused asphyxiation and they took the company to court. When the company did go to court, it eventually lost. In the process they re examined their business. What they discovered was that customers were not judging products solely on their ability to do their job. A large segment was willing to sacrifice some performance for more environmentally friendlier products.
>
> As a result of this discovery the company introduced a new line of biologically degradable cleaning products. ... Now about 45 per cent of all the company's revenue comes from these environmental friendly products.

7 Motivations for the 'Greening' of Industry - 'Insider' Views

Understanding the Range of Motivations

Given the wide range of companies involved in this study, it is not surprising that the research identified a wide range of motivating factors considered important in influencing the 'greening' of companies. These have been classified into nine broad types of motivation:

- market opportunity;
- savings from waste minimisation and resource recovery;
- avoided clean-up costs and penalties;
- environmental concern/awareness of CEO or other key individual/s;
- regulatory pressures (including legal liability);
- influence of a parent company;
- desire for a good corporate image;
- personal experience of need for the product or process; and
- other.

These categories are not mutually exclusive. For example, the desire for a good corporate image may be closely related to a company's desire to differentiate itself from its competitors and thereby gain competitive advantage/market opportunity. Likewise, regulatory pressures may be closely linked with the economic benefit of avoided penalties, and with the influence of parent companies.

It should be noted also that where terms such as 'motivations', 'beliefs', 'attitudes' and the like are used in relation to companies, there is an underlying understanding on the part of the author that these in fact equate to the 'motivations', 'beliefs', 'attitudes' etc. of key decision making personnel within companies. The following table (Table 7.1) indicates the range of motivating factors, and the extent of commonality across the companies studied.

Table 7.1: Motivating Factors Influencing the 'Greening' of Industry

Company number → Motivational factors ↓	1	2	3	4	5	6	7	8	9	10	11	12	13	14	15	16	17	18	19	20	21	22	23	24	25	26	27	28	29	30
Market opportunity	✓	✓	✓	✓	✓	✓	✓	✓	✓	✓	✓	✓	✓	✓	✓	✓	✓	✓	✓	✓	✓	✓	✓	✓	✓			✓		
Cost savings (waste minimis'n., resource recovery)						✓			✓	✓	✓	✓	✓		✓	✓					✓	✓								
Avoided clean-up costs & penalties									✓	✓				✓											✓					✓
Env'l. concern of CEO/key individual	✓	✓	✓	✓		✓		✓	✓		✓				✓				✓	✓	✓			✓	✓	✓	✓	✓	✓	✓
Regulatory pressures (incl. legal liability)						✓					✓		✓	✓		✓				✓	✓			✓						
Parent company's influence											✓		✓	✓		✓				✓				✓						
Desire for a good corporate image	✓						✓				✓		✓	✓		✓				✓				✓						✓
Knowledge of need for product or process	✓							✓			✓		✓	✓						✓				✓	✓			✓		
Other										✓																✓				

Detailed Discussion of Motivating Factors

Economic Benefits

As Table 7.1 above shows, the primary motivation for the 'greening' of industry in Australia is the economic benefits which result from that 'greening'.

Of the thirty companies studied, twenty-six indicated that the economic benefits flowing from the environmental nature of their business had been an important motivating factor. Economic benefits were seen by companies to arise in a number of different ways:

- through market opportunity and competitive advantage arising from increased community environmental awareness and/or regulatory factors;
- through cost savings resulting from waste minimisation and resource recovery and recycling;
- through avoided costs of clean-up, compensation and/or penalties associated with more environmentally damaging practices.

Market Opportunity/Competitive Advantage

Within this category of economic benefits highlighted by the companies studied were several variations in the causal factors, which broadly equate with 'consumer demand' (Blaikie & Ward 1992; Cairncross 1991; Elkington 1987; Ryan et al. 1990; Welford 1994; Worcester 1994) and 'the influence of corporate competition' (Denton 1994; Elkington & Dimmock 1991; Irvine 1991; Leighton 1992) identified through the literature.

A number of companies noted the general increase in community environmental awareness as the main reason for increased market opportunity, especially for companies manufacturing consumer products. This attitude was typified in the following statement:

> The environment is a growing market ... . It represents the way ahead, the future.

Other companies were more specific about the opportunities afforded them because of this community environmental awareness. Among these were companies which noted the potential, within this climate of environmental awareness, for companies to differentiate themselves and their products from their competitors, thereby building and maintaining market share. Through 'niche marketing', in relation to environmental benefits and health and safety benefits of their products and/or their production processes, 'green' companies are seen to be able to gain competitive advantage over other companies.

A further variation on this theme was the view, expressed by representatives of a number of companies, that not only would the companies' market share be increased in relation to their particular 'green' products or processes, but (for companies which produce a range of products, only some of which are 'green') it may also be increased more generally because of the improved corporate image resulting from 'greening'.

Stricter environmental regulation was also noted as a key factor contributing to market opportunity for 'green' companies. One company, which manufactures a machine offering safe disposal of fluorescent light tubes, was established specifically in response to new pollution regulations. Likewise, a company which manufactures insulation from waste paper, was encouraged by regulations requiring the phasing out of the use of fluorocarbons (used in the production of foam insulation - a competing product) and by regulations making insulation of new residential buildings mandatory.

Cost Savings through Waste Minimisation, Resource Recovery and Recycling

Despite the view, expressed frequently in the media, that it is unfair to expect companies to improve their environmental performance because it will cost too much, the majority of the companies studied have experienced direct economic benefits (cost savings) from their 'greening'.

As noted in the literature (Denton 1994; Smith 1991), reduced resource consumption and reduced waste disposal costs translate directly to economic gains for companies. One company, which has introduced a new, more environmentally benign method for dyeing of textiles, has benefited through reduced water consumption costs. Given the current move to user pays pricing within the water industry in Australia, this is a significant gain. The same company has also reduced its solid waste disposal costs.

Another company, which manufactures photographic equipment and supplies, has undertaken a program of resource recovery and recycling within its manufacturing plant, has also experienced significant savings. Over recent years, hazardous liquid waste requiring off-site treatment has been reduced by 25%, methanol usage has been reduced, and a recovery program for silver (a key component of the manufacturing process) which has been in operation for most of this century has continued. This has translated into direct cost savings for the company. Representatives of many of the other companies expressed similar views.

Avoided Costs of Clean-up, Compensation and Penalties

For a number of the companies studied, the potential avoidance of costs associated with the clean-up of polluted sites, compensation payments and penalties for non-compliance with environmental regulations has been an important factor motivating improved environmental performance. This supports the findings of the literature review (Bhat 1995; Brown 1995; Elkington 1987; Leighton 1992; Smith 1991; Welford 1994).

One respondent stated: "In this new era, the environment is a business issue". He went on to explain that it is better for companies to be proactive and anticipate regulations than to wait for regulations to be imposed and then have to comply:

It costs more to comply with regulations than to find voluntary solutions.

In the view of this respondent, by anticipating problems and introducing new (environmentally preferred) technology wherever possible, the company gains a competitive advantage. An example was given of a decision some years ago by the company's US arm to stop disposing of wastes through 'deep well injection', because experts within the company held the view that it was an unsustainable method of waste disposal. Its major competitor, however, continued to use the method, with the result that its corporate liabilities are now many times greater than those of this company.

Environmental Awareness/Concern of the CEO or a Key Individual

Almost half of the companies studied highlighted the environmental awareness/concern of the Chief Executive Officer of the company or another key individual in the company as an important motivating factor in the company's move to 'greenness' (Brown 1995; Elkington 1987; Ferris 1995; Leighton 1992).

For many of the companies, environmental awareness of a key individual was an important but secondary motivating factor in the 'greening' of the company. However, a number of companies indicated that the environmental awareness or concern of the CEO or another key individual was the primary motivation for 'greening', with other motivations such as economic benefit of secondary importance.

This was particularly the case where the relevant individuals' personal experiences (often childhood experiences overlaid by adult experiences) had been important in the development of that environmental awareness. For example, a founding Director of one of the small local companies studied had suffered from childhood asthma, and his awareness of air pollution issues was heightened by his difficulties with breathing. Later he lived in the USA and experienced the 'beep and creep' traffic problems in major cities there and the pollution problems of the San Francisco Bay area. The Director stated that his environmental awareness was a primary motivating factor in his choice of business direction - he co-founded a company which manufactures equipment to recover and recycle CFCs!

Similarly, one of the partners in another small local company which was part of the study, stated that personal environmental awareness was a primary motivator in the direction of the company. He spoke of his childhood in a harbourside suburb in Sydney and how he and his friends became aware over time of the gradual degradation of the environment.

> Because we lived on the water and in boats, we all saw the Harbour change. ... I can remember being able to look right through the water and it was clear and there would be seahorses and everything, and the fishermen would catch fish and that's how they lived. And then eventually everything died. Even the oysters died. The jetties, all the pylons used to be covered in oysters and now there's nothing, because of the anti-fouling paint.
>
> So ... (my) environmental awareness stems from childhood.

Overlaid on this childhood experience of environmental degradation was the respondent's experience as an adult of suffering a malignant melanoma (generally seen as aetiologically connected with environmental degradation related to ozone depletion). Whilst he states that this was not a direct motivating factor, he acknowledges it as possibly a 'sub-conscious' motivator. Considering that the products manufactured by this company are ultra-violet radiation monitors, this experience does seem likely to have been influential.

Regulatory Pressures (including Legal Liability)

The results of this study confirm the view expressed in the literature (Brown 1995; Cairncross 1991; Jacobs 1991; Leighton 1992; Ryan et al. 1990; Smith 1991; Welford 1994; Winter 1988) that pressures resulting from current or anticipated regulations and/or legislation have also been important in motivating companies to improve their environmental performance (and thereby to qualify as 'green' manufacturers).

Such pressures may be local or global. An example of the motivating force of local regulatory pressures was that experienced by the textile dyeing company mentioned above. Not only did this company experience pressure from the Environment Protection Authority (EPA) in regard to failure to meet regulations concerning emissions to air and water, but it also experienced pressure from local government in regard to contravention of regulations governing noise pollution, odours and traffic issues.

Global regulatory pressures in relation to particular incidents of environmental damage formed a powerful motivating force, particularly for larger companies operating at an international scale. Several respondents referred specifically to Bhopal, the Torrey Canyon, the Amoco Cadiz and the Exxon Valdez, and noted the heavy financial and legal liabilities which confronted companies involved in such environmentally damaging incidents. The desire to avoid the penalties experienced by other companies in relation to these well known incidents offered a great incentive to companies to improve their environmental performance.

Influence of Parent Company/Corporate Environmental Policies

One of the important motivating factors identified in the literature (Brown 1995; Leighton 1992; Schmidheiny 1992) and among the overseas-based companies studied was the influence of parent company environmental policies. An excerpt from the 1993 'Health, Safety and Environment Report' for one of these companies emphasises the importance of the parent company's environmental philosophy and policy in influencing the behaviour of subsidiary companies and their staff:

Each of these (the company's 110,000 employees worldwide) ... is responsible for promoting and protecting health, safety, and the environment.

This responsibility is seen as a basic (company) value - not just a structure that overlays manufacturing operations, but a philosophy and approach that is woven throughout the company. It is a value that impacts everything we do individually and collectively.

Such philosophies and policies have a number of different origins. For some companies, they can be traced back to the ideas or philosophy of the original founder/s of the company. In other companies, parent company environmental policies have been prompted by the social, environmental and legal context within which the parent company operates, or by economic advantages. For some companies, a number of these factors have combined to foster the development of a corporate environmental policy.

Several of the large overseas-based companies studied were founded by individuals with a strong environmental and/or social ethic. This has flowed through into corporate philosophy and policy, and has been a key factor influencing the environmental behaviour of the Australian subsidiary companies.

For example, one of the companies studied was founded in the late 19th century in Germany by an individual who was a leader in the areas of industrial reform and human rights. When the founder died, the company was (in accordance with the founder's instructions) set up as a family trust with conditions requiring that 90% of company profits after tax must be either invested in research and development or given to charity. Environmental concern is seen within the company as a natural flow-on from the corporate philosophy as established by the founder. This environmental concern has been reinforced by the prevailing social, environmental and legal conditions in Germany. There, widespread community concern about the environmental impacts of pollution (for example) have resulted in strong social and regulatory pressures being placed on companies to improve their environmental performance. Since the Australian company is a wholly owned subsidiary of the German company, there is strong pressure on it to conform with parent company environmental standards.

The integral nature of environmental concern to the whole philosophical basis of another of the overseas-based companies (founded in the United Kingdom in the 1970s) is summed up in this quote from a member of the Environment, Health and Safety Department of the company:

> I think if you'd spoken to (the founder) seventeen years ago, she wouldn't have said 'I am about to found a green company'. She was just about to found a company based on her own principles, which were 'don't waste'. And as the environmental movement has grown up, those have merged. And I think as the whole company took off, the environment became part of its founding, its centrepoints, because that was one of the things that (the founder) cared about: she cares about the environment, she cares about human rights, she cares about animal welfare. And I don't think it's ever ... been 'inserted in' - it's just been a part of the overall whole attitude and philosophy ... the whole ethos.

The origin of parent company environmental policy in other of the overseas-based companies is in response to contextual factors affecting the parent company. For example, according to key informants within an Australian automobile manufacturing company which is a wholly-owned subsidiary of a USA company, the corporate directives from the company's head office in USA which influence environmental improvements within the Australian company are strongly influenced by the legal context within the USA, including the threat of litigation and the requirement for the company to act with 'due diligence'.

Corporate Image

Desire for a good corporate image is also an important motivating factor in the 'greening' of industry. This particularly applies to established companies (rather than to new companies), and especially to large companies operating at an international level (Elkington 1987; Elkington & Dimmock 1991). This relates not only to the company's corporate image with its customers, but also with its neighbours, with regulators and with the community at large.

Among those interviewed for this study, a commonly used phrase was 'the company's desire to be seen to be doing the right thing'. In some cases, this has been prompted by an awareness that there is a competitive advantage in a good corporate image. In others, it has been prompted by the realisation that a good corporate image will result in the company having more freedom to regulate itself within defined parameters (as in the Victorian EPA licensing system).

In one company, it was the realisation that the company's poor corporate image in relation to environmental issues was hampering staff recruitment and lowering staff morale which prompted action to improve that image. During the 1960s and 1970s, the company was involved in some high profile damaging environmental issues. The company's involvement in the production of napalm and agent orange used during the Vietnam war badly damaged the company's reputation and seriously undermined the morale of the company's employees. As a result, the company had difficulty recruiting graduates to work within the company. However, the extent to which its reputation had been damaged was not appreciated until staff recruitment officers from the company visiting two universities were greeted by open hostility. In one university in New Zealand, they were faced with skull and crossbones signs displayed on every desk. In the USA during the time of the Vietnam War the company's recruiters visiting one university were locked in a room which was then set on fire.

Personal Experience of Need for the Product or Process

For at least seven of the companies studied, personal experience of need for the product or process has been an important motivating factor in the development of their products or processes. No parallel motivation was found in the literature. However, there is some similarity between this factor and the issue raised by Elkington (1987) concerning CEOs' personal awareness of environmental problems.

Although closely related to the earlier category of 'market opportunity', this is really a more basic motivating force. Whereas 'market opportunity' indicates that the individual or company has identified the potential for the product to fill a gap in the market, 'personal experience of need' relates to the individual's own need for the product or process. Such a need may later give rise to the identification of market opportunity, but for these individuals/companies it was the personal experience which preceded such an identification.

The companies for which this was a motivating factor vary hugely in size, success level and market sector. Not surprisingly, three of the smallest companies indicated that personal experience of need was a primary motivating force for them.

The manufacturer of a polluted-water separator for use with rainwater tanks developed the product primarily to improve the water quality at his rural Victorian property. Likewise, the developer of a machine for the direct seeding of trees developed the product in order to redress the declining sustainability of his own farming land, due to loss of trees.

For some of the companies, not only was personal need a motivating factor in the development of their products and/or processes, but also in the establishment of the companies themselves. This was true for one of the larger companies - an overseas-based company which manufactures and retails cosmetics using naturally-based ingredients. According to the company's founder, her experience as a purchaser was a key motivating factor in the establishment of the company itself and in the design of the company's products. In her autobiography, she states:

> It seemed ridiculous to me that you could go into a sweet shop and ask for an ounce of jelly babies and you could go into the grocer's and ask for two ounces of cheese, but when you wanted to buy a body lotion you had to go in to Boots' and lay out five quid for a bloody great bottle of the stuff. Then, if you didn't like it, you were stuck with it.
>
> ... Why couldn't I buy cosmetics by weight or bulk, like I could if I wanted groceries or vegetables? Why couldn't I buy a small size of a cream or a lotion, so I could try it out before buying a big bottle? ...
>
> It was also obvious to anyone who thought about it that a lot of the cost of cosmetics was down to fancy packaging. That was another source of deep irritation to me. When I bought perfume all I cared about was what it smelled like. I didn't give a damn about what the bottle looked like, and furthermore I did not know any women who did. We all suspected we were being conned, but there was precious little we could do about it.
>
> I sat down and discussed it with Gordon, telling him the kind of shop I was thinking of opening was one that sold cosmetics products in different sizes and in cheap containers.

Other Motivating Factors

In seven of the companies studied, there were motivating factors which fell outside the range described above. Most of these factors were noted by only one or two companies. They included:

- occupational health and safety issues (for example, the health effects of chlorine bleaching), which prompted companies to look for other ways of producing their products;
- the nature of the business, which encourages clean production because of the danger contamination poses to the company's products;
- the international nature of business, requiring companies to apply a common high standard of environmental performance in all their plants across the globe to avoid having a range of different standards in different branches and the difficulties that would pose;
- awareness of resource limitations raised by the 1970s oil crisis;
- community expectations that companies will respond appropriately to environmental challenges;
- the influence of 'green activism' on community attitudes and corporate image; and
- the intellectual challenge of addressing a problem previously unsolved.

Comparison of Motivations as Identified through Study Findings and Existing Literature

Whilst the majority of motivational factors identified through this study are those commonly cited as reasons for the 'greening' of industry, several of the key motivating factors identified through this study are rarely, if ever, referred to in current literature. These relate to the personal experience and/or personal awareness of key individuals within companies. They are:

- the environmental concern/awareness of the CEO or other key individuals;
- personal experience of need for the product; and
- personal experience of the need for improvement in corporate image.

The influence of these personal factors is not limited (as might perhaps be expected) to the smaller companies in the study, but occurs in large and small companies alike. However, it is more common in the smaller companies than in those which are large.

Leighton (1992) and Schmidheiny (1992) both highlight the case of the chairperson of Du Pont (Ed Woolard Jr.) who considered that the abbreviation 'CEO' stood not only for 'Chief Executive Officer' but also for 'Chief Environmental Officer'. However, in the bulk of the literature, the environmental concern/awareness and personal commitment of company leaders has not featured regularly among the motivations cited for the greening of industry.

Another important distinction can be drawn between the existing literature and the findings of this study concerning the basis for that environmental concern/awareness/commitment.   Existing literature generally asserts that where such an attitude exists, it is the result of the age of the individual concerned. Leighton (1992 p.29) refers to "the sixties culture" and links the pro-environment attitudes of some industry leaders to the fact that they grew up in that era. Whilst that link has also been highlighted as important by some of the respondents to this study, perhaps more important for many have been their personal experiences relating to the environment or environmental problems.

For example, one company director highlighted as a key motivating factor the problems he experienced with childhood asthma, which he linked to the proliferation of chemical sprays being used in the fruit-growing area in which he grew up. Another remembered having an uncle who had suffered serious medical problems linked to an accumulation of farm chemical residues in his body, and indicated that this had influenced him strongly.   Several others noted childhood experiences of the environment which had heightened their environmental awareness.

One respondent commented on observing as a child the gradual disappearance of marine life in Sydney Harbour. The same person noted that, when living in Italy in the 1980s he and his family had met up with some German doctors and he had mentioned the family's intention to travel north to Finland. The Germans had warned them not to take children up there, because they had been dealing with children who suffered exposure to radiation as a result of the Chernobyl nuclear accident, and said the problem was getting worse rather than better. That experience, together with his later personal experience with melanoma, had proved an important motivating factor in his establishment of a company which manufactures personal ultra-violet radiation monitors.

Another distinction which can be drawn between existing literature and the findings of this study is related to the desire for a good corporate image. Much of the literature focuses on corporate competition as the genesis of this concern over corporate image. Other literature highlights the pressure from within companies, from their employees, to improve their environmental performance as an important motivator. For example, Leighton (1992 p.30) says:

> Executives run companies but common people make them work. And common people are showing less and less tolerance for environmentally irresponsible companies. People don't leave their convictions with the receptionist when they come to work in the morning. This explains the enthusiasm most employees show for corporate recycling initiatives .... .

However, one company included in this study highlighted a rationale for improving corporate image which stands out starkly from the rest: that of fear for personal safety. During the 1960s and 1970s, the company was involved in the production of napalm and agent orange used during the Vietnam war. As a result of litigation over this issue, the company's reputation was badly damaged and the morale of its workforce was seriously undermined. In turn, the company had difficulty in recruiting graduates for its workforce. Seeking to address this problem, the company's recruiters visited universities around USA and in other countries. On a visit to one American university, the company's recruiters found themselves locked in a room which was then set on fire. As the Manager, Environment, Health and Safety for the Australian subsidiary company stated, this incident brought home to the company the extent to which its image had been damaged.

A common thread running through each of these examples from this study is the importance of personal threat as a motivator. However, whilst in existing literature personal environmental threat has not been commonly linked with the greening of industry, it has been linked to personal environmental practices (Baldassare & Katz 1992). In their article entitled 'The Personal Threat of Environmental Problems as Predictor of Environmental Practices', Baldassare and Katz (1992 p.612) state:

> The results indicate that personal environmental threat affects overall environmental practices in a more significant way than either political or demographic variables.

Interestingly, although implied to some extent in the other motivating factors mentioned by study respondents, several of the key motivating factors identified in the literature have not been identified specifically by participating companies. These include: awareness/recognition of environmental problems; the development of full-cost accounting; and the influence of environmentalists. To some extent this is not surprising.

As noted in the literature, "awareness of the existence of environmental problems is, on its own, not enough to motivate the vast majority of people to take action" (Winter 1988 p.17). Likewise, the nascent system of full-cost accounting is as yet insufficiently developed to motivate corporate environmentalism to any great degree. Whilst it is likely that environmentalists have influenced corporate behaviour through their influence on individuals, little evidence was found of active links between the environmental movement and industry in Australia, so the lack of acknowledgment of environmentalists' influence is not remarkable.

Overview of 'Outsider' and 'Insider' Views on Motivations for the 'Greening' of Industry

Whilst an overwhelming majority of company executives acknowledge the importance of 'structural' factors such as economic constraints and opportunities, and regulatory frameworks in motivating or influencing their 'greening', many also acknowledge the importance of their own or other individuals' decisions, choices and actions.

Companies have been motivated by the opportunities for competitive advantage afforded by 'greening', as well as by savings which can be made through reductions in resource consumption, waste disposal costs, clean-up costs, compensation payouts and penalties.

Regulatory pressures have also been identified as an important motivating factor for the 'greening' of companies. In order to avoid penalties for failure to meet regulated standards, companies may adopt 'green' practices. An interesting 'spin-off' effect is that companies which have complied with strict regulations or have voluntarily met strict environmental standards often encourage broader application of such standards. In this way, regulatory pressures may be seen as both the 'medium' and the 'outcome' of the 'greening' of industry (demonstrating Giddens' concept of 'the duality of structure').

However the fact that, within a given set of economic and regulatory frameworks, there are companies which have adopted 'green' processes and/or products and others which have not indicates the importance of an additional factor: choice or will (which Giddens terms 'agency'). For almost half of the companies in this study, choice or will, based particularly on the environmental awareness or concern of a key individual, was an important motivating factor in their 'greening'. Another factor underlying the choice of companies in this study to adopt 'green' products/processes was the personal experience by a key individual of need for the product/process. Although it is fair to say that this closely relates to market opportunity (and in that sense can be seen as a 'structural' factor in companies' 'greening'), there is clearly an element of choice or will involved in the decision to take up that opportunity, and there is an individual aspect to the identification of the need.

Desire for a good corporate image was another important motivating factor identified through this study, particularly relating to the large established companies rather than to smaller nascent companies. Where such companies find their reputations tarnished by past environmental 'misdemeanours', the effects on companies may be damaging both economically and in terms of morale. They may adopt 'green' processes as one way of improving their image with neighbours, regulators and the community. The example cited demonstrates Giddens' concept of 'reflexive monitoring of actions', and shows how such a process may be an important factor in the transformation of companies in respect of environmental behaviour.

In general, within the study sample, the larger corporations (particularly the long established, transnational companies or large Australian companies which have substantial overseas activities) appear to be more likely to be motivated by factors such as regulatory pressures and the threat of legal liability than by the personal experience or attitudes of a key individual. By contrast, smaller local companies (especially those with key individuals who have a high level of awareness of environmental issues) are more likely to be motivated by personal environmental concern than by external pressures. This difference may be the result of the nature of large institutions, in which the concerns and views of an individual are easily lost or overrun by other factors, reflecting Giddens' view that "the more ... institutions bite into time and space - the more resistant they are to manipulation or change by any individual agent". (Giddens 1984 p.377)

As indicated earlier in this book, the findings of this study are based largely on the views expressed by key informants from the companies. They therefore reflect the perceptions and understandings of those individuals concerning the motivations and influences on company decision making, which may not reflect accurately in all cases the actual motivations and influences. Moreover, even where the information was provided by the actual decision-maker, it is possible that underlying motivations (of which the individual was not conscious but which nevertheless affected the decision) were overlooked. Several of the companies studied show evidence of 'unconscious motivations' as distinct from their conscious motivations. For example, the director of the small local company which manufactures personal ultra-violet radiation monitors acknowledges that, although not a direct and conscious motivation for the development of the product, his experience of suffering melanoma was possibly a 'sub-conscious' motivating factor. Another example is the large UK-based franchise company for which the conscious motivation was the development of a company which would sell affordable products in appropriate quantities. However, an important underlying ('unconscious') motivation was personal concern for the environment on the part of the company's founder.

8   Help from Inside and Outside - Factors Assisting the 'Greening' of Industry

The Nature and Relevance of Factors Assisting Companies

Factors assisting the 'greening' of companies have been identified, and these have been classified as 'internal' and 'external' factors. However, to some extent, the division between the categories is arbitrary, as some 'internal' factors are derived from earlier 'external' influences. 'Internal' factors are defined as those arising from within the company itself, whereas 'external' factors are those which impinge on the company from outside.

Although most respondents identified both internal and external factors which had assisted their company, one respondent indicated that nothing had assisted his company. Not surprisingly, this was one of the companies which was judged to have had a low level of success.

Help from Inside - Internal Factors Assisting Companies

Nine broad types of internal factors assisting companies were identified:

- business skills and experience of management and senior staff;
- structure/functioning of the company;
- access to capital;
- commitment of key staff;
- internal impacts of being part of a multinational corporation;
- benefits of product/process;
- prior activities of organisation;
- the 1960s and 1970s culture of key individuals; and
- other internal factors.

Table 8.1 indicates the range of internal factors assisting companies and the spread of these across the sample of companies.

Table 8.1: Internal Factors Assisting the 'Greening' of Industry

Company number → Factors ↓	1	2	3	4	5	6	7	8	9	10	11	12	13	14	15	16	17	18	19	20	21	22	23	24	25	26	27	28	29	30
Skills & expertise of managem't & staff	✓	✓	✓	✓	✓	✓	✓						✓	✓	✓	✓				✓	✓	✓					✓	✓	✓	✓
Access to capital	✓																								✓					
Size, structure & functioning of co.	✓	✓	✓										✓							✓							✓			
Commitment of key staff													✓							✓							✓			
Being part of a multinational corp'n.													✓							✓						✓				
Benefits of product or process									✓				✓														✓			
Prior activities of the organisation/comp'y.													✓							✓										✓
1960s and 1970s culture of key indivs.											✓															✓				
Other								✓																						✓

Business Skills and Experience of Management and Senior Staff

By far the most common factor said to have assisted companies to succeed as 'green' businesses was the skill or expertise of management and/or staff. These skills included business management skills, as well as technical expertise and 'networking' skills (ie. the ability to establish beneficial links with other relevant organisations). This is backed up by the literature which notes the lack of such skills and experience as a major hindrance to 'green' industry (McKinsey 1993; Pappas et al. 1990).

Almost two-thirds of the companies noted the business management skills and experience of the CEO as an important factor. In many cases, it was the understanding of cash flow issues which was most helpful, especially in the early and intermediate stages of the establishment of companies. One executive commented that understanding of the importance of business plans and of good management, knowledge about cash flow issues, and awareness of the constraints affecting the market are all critical factors in the success of companies (whether 'green' or not).

Technical expertise was also highlighted as important. For example, an executive of one company in the study noted the importance of the technical skills of the CEO (who is trained in applied biology) in developing an appropriate formulation for the company's product. Another company has as its 'Environment Manager' a person who was previously a senior staff member within the relevant State environmental regulatory agency. By drawing on his experience and knowledge, the company has been able to influence government policy makers to take account of the needs of business in the framing of relevant environmental regulations.

Both technical expertise and an understanding of the issues confronting those who will provide the market for the product were highlighted as important by an executive of a company which manufactures a product for the agricultural market. He noted that while his technical skill enabled him to identify the particular environmental problem and develop a solution for it, his ability to empathise with the farmers who might use the product was also important as it enabled him to develop a product which was appropriate (and, therefore, more likely to be successful). This reflects, to some extent, the point raised by Hawken (1993 p.138) concerning the nature of small business as an advantage ("they are closer to their customers").

Networking links with relevant individuals and organisations were also noted as important. An example of 'networking' highlighted in the study was a company in which one partner had formerly been the financial editor of a large metropolitan daily newspaper and was able to use his contacts to access capital for the business, and the other partner had lived and worked in the USA and was able to use his contacts to gain access to the US market for the company's product. These were both important factors in the company's success.

Structure/Functioning of the Company

The second most commonly cited factor assisting companies was the structure and functioning of the companies themselves. This particularly related to the ability of the company structure to facilitate quick decision-making, although one company also highlighted the flexibility gained by using sub-contractors for some of its manufacturing. In keeping with the findings of the literature review that there are advantages for small business which relate to their size, structure and functioning (Hawken 1993), it was the smaller local companies which raised this issue, rather than the larger and/or multinational corporations.

One executive referred to the "short chain of command" and the "flat" structure of his company as being critical to the company's success. In his view, this system (in which the CEO has ultimate responsibility but other senior management have considerable autonomy) not only enables quick decisions, but also provides staff with a sense that they have a significant part to play and thereby draws a high level of staff commitment.

Access to Capital

Access to capital has been identified through the literature as critical to the success of industry (including 'green' industry) (Baden & Stroup 1991).

Internal access to capital (ie. the existence within the company of an adequate capital base) was cited by executives of three companies as a factor which had assisted their companies to succeed. As one CEO noted, "you can go broke making a profit". He pointed out that there is a need for a reasonable capital base to see companies through the lag time between manufacturing, packaging and distributing the product and actually receiving payment for it. Where such a capital base exists, companies are able to sustain (and even expand) their production as required.

Commitment of Key Staff

Another key factor in the success of companies, highlighted through this study, was the level of commitment of key staff (and, indeed, of staff in general). This view is supported by the literature (Clarke 1995; Denton 1994; Hay et al. 1989; Leighton 1992; Pearce 1991; Schmidheiny 1992).

Among the companies studied, both the commitment of the Managing Director or Chief Executive Officer and the commitment of other staff were cited as factors contributing to the success of companies. For example, one of the smaller locally-based companies noted as important two aspects of commitment: the strength of commitment of the CEO, arising from his spiritually-based concern for the welfare of humanity and the environment; and the commitment of the staff to the ethos and ideals of the company.

A larger overseas-based company highlighted the importance of the involvement of employees in identifying opportunities for improved environmental performance, and the commitment of employees to this (perhaps enhanced by the provision of a $200 monthly award for the best suggestion for reducing the company's environmental impact). The same company was one of a number of the larger overseas-based companies which noted the importance of high-level commitment, such as by the CEO.

One of the large Australian companies highlighted the importance of raising the profile of environmental issues in the company by establishing environmental roles and responsibilities at high levels of the organisation rather than at site level (as had previously been the case in the company), and thereby raising the overall company commitment to environmental issues.

Impacts of Being Part of a Multinational Corporation

The literature reviewed for this study makes no direct reference to multinationalism of corporations as a factor affecting their success or failure. However, there are some references which relate indirectly to this issue.

The availability of greater levels of capital in multinational corporations (alluded to by Baden & Stroup 1991; McKinsey 1993) is confirmed by two companies. One noted the importance of the availability of large sums of money within the international corporation for research and development, enabling the company to develop more environmentally sound technology. The other noted the support of the parent company in providing funding for environmental monitoring.

From the literature, a number of other aspects of multinationalism which facilitate the 'greening' of industry can also be identified. These include the heightened awareness within multinational companies of the threats posed to companies by environmental accidents and of environmental issues in general (Brown 1995; Smith 1991; Winter 1988) and the ready availability of a substantial market (Elkington 1987; McKinsey 1993; Saddler 1990).

These have been acknowledged by six of the overseas-based companies and the large Australian companies in this study as important factors in their success as 'green' companies. One overseas-based company cited three aspects of the company's multinationalism as important in helping the successful 'greening' of the Australian company. The first was the heightened awareness of environmental issues within the global company resulting from the environmental situation in the countries or regions in which the company originated (Europe) and operates (worldwide). The second was the existence within the parent company of committees and documentation providing guidance on environmental issues. The third was the requirements of the parent company that the Australian operation report bi-annually to this committee on the Australian company's environmental performance. Another company cited the links with the multinational parent company as being important in gaining access to markets to which it would otherwise have been difficult to gain entry.

Benefits of Product/Process

Although there is no reference to it in the literature, another important aid to the 'greening' of companies in this study was to do with the products they are manufacturing.

One CEO expressed the view that even if a product is environmentally sound, unless it "stacks up economically" it will not succeed in the marketplace. His company had succeeded because its products 'stacked up'. This economic viability of products was mentioned by several other companies as well. For another company, the reasons for success included not only the economic advantages of the company's product over its competitors, but also the uniqueness of the product, meaning it has no direct competition.

Among the overseas-based companies, one highlighted a number of product-based reasons for the company's success. These included: the quality of the products; the fact that the claims made for the products are believable; and the minimal packaging and the reuse of containers, both of which appeal to customers.

Prior Activities of Organisation

Another factor assisting companies included in this study has also not appeared in the literature: the effect of prior activities of the organisation in enhancing the organisation's ability to move into 'green' manufacturing.

For example, the Australian subsidiary of a large overseas-based company had recently upgraded its facilities, which enabled it to respond quickly to the need for 'greener' products. Another large overseas-based company had implemented a quality assurance program within its Australian operation, which enabled it to monitor its environmental performance more effectively, and therefore to take steps to improve it.

Two other large overseas-based companies also noted the importance of prior activities in their successful 'greening'. One highlighted the influence of the development in 1991 of a company environmental policy, which communicated the importance of environmental management and helped focus attention within the various elements of the company on the environmental impacts of their activities. For the other company, the prior activity which helped the company in its environmental activities was the good reputation which the company has established over time with regulatory bodies such as the EPA. This has resulted in the company being granted 'bubble licences' which have allowed the company to achieve its improved environmental performance in ways which cause the least disbenefit to the company.

The 1960s and 1970s Culture of Key Individuals

In keeping with the literature (Elkington 1987; Leighton 1992), the persistence within key individuals of the culture of the 1960s and 1970s was identified as an important factor influencing the success of several companies in this study.

One of the small local companies has highlighted as important in the successful development of its product the fact that the inventor grew up in the 1960s and 1970s. In the view of the inventor, the 1960s and 1970s were times which developed creativity, whereas (in his view) the 1980s and 1990s are not. He stated:

> I see younger people now as being incredibly conservative. It's probably to do with the times they live in, with such insecurity. I don't think it's any accident that the great software inventors are all in their mid forties. ... I guess we all came through an extraordinary time.

For one of the large overseas-based companies, the influence of the 1960s was also important. The fact that the company's founder grew up in the 1960s was important both in the direction of the company's development and in its success, as it engendered a passion to fulfil the company's potential. As the founder stated in her autobiography:

> For someone like myself, whose thinking was forged in the sixties, it was a magical prospect. The very notion of using a business as a crusader, of harnessing success to ideals, set my imagination on fire. From that moment (the company) ceased to exist, at least in my eyes, as just another trading business. It became a force for social change. It became a lobby group to campaign on environmental and human rights issues. It became a communicator and an educator.

Other Internal Factors

Two other internal factors have been identified by companies in this study as assisting in their success. Both relate to very small local companies, and both have a time dimension to them. For one company, the successful development of its product had been associated with a decline in the inventor's other business due to the recession, resulting in more time being available to him to work on his invention. The success of the other company has been aided by the willingness of staff to operate on a part-time basis, enabling the company to keep the cost of its product down to a reasonable level and thereby to maintain market dominance.

Help from Outside - External Factors Assisting Companies

Table 8.2 indicates the range of external factors assisting companies and the spread of these across the sample of companies.

Table 8.2:   External Factors Assisting the 'Greening' of Industry

Factors ↓ / Company number →	1	2	3	4	5	6	7	8	9	10	11	12	13	14	15	16	17	18	19	20	21	22	23	24	25	26	27	28	29	30
Access to investment funds	✓	✓																												
Government support (grants, loans, etc.)				✓	✓	✓								✓					✓											
Legislation, regulations, licensing conditions				✓										✓				✓						✓		✓				
Links with other organisations	✓													✓				✓					✓		✓	✓	✓			
Community awareness of environmental issues						✓								✓				✓							✓				✓	
Economic climate and/or pressures						✓	✓											✓				✓								
Australia's culture of innovation																						✓		✓						
Serendipity	✓													✓				✓										✓		✓
Other					✓													✓										✓		

Nine broad classifications of 'external' factors assisting companies to succeed as 'green' manufacturers have been identified. They are:

- links with/support from other organisations;
- community awareness of environmental issues;
- government support (in the form of grants, loans, etc.);
- legislation/regulations/licensing conditions;
- economic climate and/or economic pressures;
- 'serendipity';
- Australia's culture of innovation;
- access to capital/availability of investment funds; and
- other.

Links with/Support from Other Organisations

The most commonly cited external factor assisting companies in the study was the links which companies have formed with other organisations. This accords with the findings from the literature review (Brown 1995; Elkington 1987; Leighton 1992; Marsh 1991; Nash & Ehrenfeld 1996; Schmidheiny 1992).   Relevant links include those with peak industry bodies, environmental groups, advisory and/or regulatory bodies, and other business entities.

One locally-based company cited the advantage it had received from previously established connections with a major retailing chain, which resulted in ready access to markets for its 'green' product.

Two companies noted the importance of the knowledge, contacts, encouragement, publicity and prize money gained through their participation in government-sponsored 'Enterprise Workshops' run through business management departments of educational institutions.   Another highlighted the importance of the encouragement received through the winning of environmental awards.

For three other companies, the important links were with organisations such as semi-government instrumentalities (eg. the State Electricity Commission of Victoria - now Electricity Services Victoria), which provided advice and assistance with product promotion.

One company highlighted the importance of the support it received from a government research agency which demonstrated the benefits of the company's product and established a system of certification, monitoring and quality control.   This encouraged acceptance of the product by the market and thereby contributed to the company's success.

Another company highlighted the importance of membership of industry-based groups such as the Plastics and Chemical Industries Association (formerly the Australian Chemical Industry Council) which has involved the company in the 'Responsible Care' program and has provided valuable guidance and information.

Links with and support from environmental groups were noted by two companies as important to their 'successful greening'. For example, one company noted that support from groups such as the Australian Conservation Foundation and the Worldwide Fund for Nature has encouraged the company to promote its products as 'environmentally preferred'. It has also given the company confidence to be open to criticism from environmental groups and to see such criticism as a means of identifying problems which it can then resolve, rather than seeing the criticism itself as a problem. This relationship with such groups thereby provides the company with an 'edge', not just in marketing terms but also in terms of environmental awareness. A similar view was expressed by an executive of another company.

Close liaison with environmental regulators has also been identified by companies in this study as an important factor in their successful 'greening'. Executives of one company gave the example of the negotiation of a licence agreement between the company and a regulatory body in which the company lodged a bond of 12% of the cost of proposed environmental works as a surety for certain pollution reduction projects. This provided benefits both to the regulatory authority (in the form of a company commitment to environmental improvements) and to the company (in terms of additional time to investigate and remedy environmental problems). The arrangement offered an incentive for the company to complete the works, as the money would otherwise be forfeited.

Community Awareness of Environmental Issues

Growing community environmental awareness, both in Australia and overseas, has been an important factor in the successful 'greening' of industry (Cairncross 1991; Elkington 1987; Leighton 1992; Welford 1994; Winter 1988).

For example, the CEO of one small locally-based company manufacturing insulation from waste paper highlighted the importance to the company's initial success of the high level of awareness by Australians concerning the value of insulation in housing. During the energy crisis of the late 1970s, this awareness had been fostered through advertising campaigns such as those undertaken by the State Electricity Commission of Victoria and the Gas and Fuel Corporation, encouraging householders to install insulation as a means of saving on fuel costs.

Other companies supported this view. For example, an executive from one large overseas-based company drew attention to the publicity given in the media to the environment (including 'lifestyle programs' promoting mulching, recycling and reuse), and the role this has played in heightened awareness of environmental issues worldwide. This has been reinforced (according to this executive) by greater global communication and greater education on environmental issues. As a result, both the companies which manufacture consumer products and the consumers who use them are more informed about and interested in the impacts of those products on the environment. This benefits companies which are taking steps to reduce negative environmental impacts from their products and/or processes.

Similar views were expressed by an executive of a company which manufactures solar (photovoltaic) cells. He highlighted the importance of publicity given to such events as the annual solar car race, together with increased solar energy education in schools, in promoting community awareness of solar energy and creating an increase in the market for solar cells.

Government Support (in the Form of Grants, Loans, etc.)

Although there is no reference to it in the literature, according to respondents in this study, the provision of government support for the 'greening' of industry has been an important factor in companies' success. This is especially true for the smaller locally-based companies.

One company acknowledged the importance of a Federal Government grant towards the cost of developing and patenting a prototype of the company's product (a machine for recovering and recycling refrigerants from automotive air-conditioning systems). However, the CEO did point out that by the time the money was actually paid, the prototype was almost finished.

Another company highlighted the importance of the support it received from the National Industry Extension Scheme, in the form of a

50% subsidy towards the cost of developing a business plan, in ensuring that the business had a solid basis on which to build.

Austrade was identified by one company as a source of significant assistance, both through its 'Project Marketing Loans' and through the provision of low cost market research. According to the company's CEO, Austrade has recognised the inability of (small) companies to obtain finance from banks for export market development, and has developed a system whereby if a company has a product which can be exported it can obtain a loan from Austrade to facilitate that process. One problem with the 'Project Marketing Loans' scheme, according to the CEO, is that only half of the money is paid 'up front', with the remainder being reimbursed by Austrade (still as a loan) once evidence is provided of the expenditure of the full amount. For many small businesses, this creates an insurmountable cash flow problem. A second problem with the scheme (in the view of the CEO) is the condition governing repayment of funds by businesses (having been assessed by Austrade as likely to achieve their projected levels of export earnings). If companies are successful in achieving their export goals, 100% of the loan is repayable. By contrast, if companies do not achieve their goals, then only 50% of the loan is repayable. This is positive in that it encourages companies to 'take the plunge', but it can also be seen as an incentive for some companies to give up before achieving their export goals. Nevertheless, in the view of the CEO, the scheme is a significant step forward for small businesses attempting to enter the export market.

Other loans, grants and subsidies received by companies in this study, and which were held by those companies to be important in their successful 'greening' included:

- a grant from the Victorian Government under its Clean Technology Incentive Scheme for the purchase of equipment, which was acknowledged by one company as an important factor in the successful establishment of its cleaner production process;
- an interest-free Cleaner Production Loan from the EPA to enable one company to establish a working demonstration facility and to show potential customers the benefits of the company's technology, was acknowledged by the company as "the single most valuable piece of assistance received by the company from government"; and
- the provision of government subsidies for the purchase of solar cells by people setting up Remote Area Power Supply schemes has been an

important form of indirect assistance to the company which manufactures solar photovoltaic cells.

Legislation/Regulations/Licensing Conditions

In keeping with the findings of the literature review (Cairncross 1991; Jacobs 1991; Leighton 1992; Ryan et al. 1990), the combined impacts of legislation, regulations and licensing conditions have been an important external form of assistance to the 'green' companies in this study.

Six companies noted the fact that government legislation had created or expanded the markets for their products. For example, the company which manufactures machinery to recover and recycle the refrigerants from automotive air conditioning systems drew attention to the importance to its success of the Victorian legislation to control emissions of CFCs. Similarly, the company which manufactures the equipment for removal of asbestos, has been assisted by the requirement that every company in Australia with premises contaminated with asbestos must have the premises audited by an occupational hygienist, and must then lodge with the relevant Occupational Health and Safety Authority its plan for addressing the contamination problem. This means, of course, that the company has a 'captive' market. The threat of litigation against companies which fail to address their asbestos contamination problems reinforces this market opportunity.

The importance of this threat of litigation (not only in respect of asbestos contamination, but in terms of general environmental damage) has been confirmed by a number of the companies studied. One CEO stated:

> One of the things that is really driving environmental concerns is the fact that directors can be thrown into gaol for negligence. Now *that* all of a sudden takes the problem all the way to the General Manager and the Board of Directors. In the past (their attitude has) always been to tell managers: 'that's not going to impact us - find a way to cause the problem to go away without spending money'. But now they know that if they use that sort of technique and in fact they cause damage to the environment they are personally liable.

An executive of another company - one of the large overseas-based companies which has adopted 'greener' processes in its manufacturing - indicated that incidents such as Bhopal have reinforced the company's awareness of the legal and financial liabilities resulting from poor environmental management.

However, it is not just past environmental incidents and litigation or current legislative frameworks that encourage companies to adopt 'greener' technologies. One executive noted that there is a growing awareness in the corporate sector that even if there are not environmental controls in place now, they will be instigated in the future. Therefore the threat of future legislation or litigation can influence the choice of technology by companies when they are setting up, expanding or up-grading.

The importance of the influence of overseas legislation was highlighted by an executive from one of the large overseas-based companies, which manufactures computers. He indicated that once the German legislation came in placing the onus on the manufacturer to take back the machine at the end of its life, the company adopted that approach world-wide.

Licensing conditions have also had an important influence on companies in this study. The negotiation of 'bubble licences' has already been discussed. In addition, one company which manufactures biological products to remediate problems of air and soil pollution acknowledged the importance of the cost of EPA discharge licences being linked to the amount of pollution discharged. This emphasises the benefits of reducing pollution and enhances the take up of technology such as this company manufactures.

Economic Climate and/or Economic Pressures

The literature indicates that economic factors have an important influence on environmental behaviour (Denton 1994; Elkington 1987; Irvine 1991; Leighton 1992). For companies in this study, economic factors have both motivated and assisted companies in their 'greening'.

Five companies noted the assistance they received from the economic recession experienced in Australia in recent years. The CEO of one company stated that the recession had highlighted the need for product differentiation in order to sustain market share. For another company, the recession reduced relatively the costs of the upgrading of the company's facilities. This was a necessary precursor to the company's improved environmental performance.

In several companies, the recent tight economic conditions prompted closer examination of processes to identify any potential savings from resource recovery and/or waste minimisation. For one company in particular, this tendency was reinforced by the escalating costs of waste disposal in Sydney, where the company's Australian headquarters is located.

'Serendipity'

'Serendipity' is defined by Collins English Dictionary as "the faculty of making fortunate discoveries by accident" (Hanks et al. 1979 p.1330). According to Hanks et al. (p.1330) it is an 18th Century term which was "coined by Horace Walpole from the Persian fairytale *The Three Princes of Serendip*, in which the heroes possess this gift". Serendipity receives relatively little attention in the literature on industrial environmentalism, although it is alluded to by several of the works reviewed for this study (Clarke 1995; Hawken 1993). However, for a number of the companies in this study it has been an important factor assisting their 'greening'.

The following narrative of the history of one company's entry into the world of 'green manufacturing' underlines the importance of serendipity.

A Case of ... 'Serendipity'

Originally, the company was involved in meat exporting. However, due to the erosion of markets (resulting from competition from other meat exporting countries and from the strengthening of the Australian dollar), they were slowly but surely 'going broke'. The fact that the former CEO had recently completed an economics degree, in which he had learned something of barter trading, was the first of a series of 'coincidences' (serendipitous events) in this saga. He decided to give the barter trading a try, since with empty containers coming back to Australia the shipping costs would be minimal, and began looking around for a suitable product with which the meat could be traded. Through this process, the company became involved in barter trading with China - bringing frozen spring rolls back in the containers which had been used to carry the meat. That arrangement worked well until the Chinese manufacturer of the spring rolls changed the formulation of the rolls, with the result that the new rolls exploded when cooked.

With a debt to the company of over $800,000, the Beijing area officials (with whom the company had been dealing) were anxious to find a replacement product which could be traded for the meat. The substitute product they offered was incandescent light globes.

The timing of this offer of light globes is another 'coincidence'. This was the late 1980s, when supermarket chains and discount stores were moving towards having their own house brands of items such as light globes. They (the chains) had asked the big companies manufacturing or importing light globes to supply them with globes under the house brand, but the big companies had refused initially, because of a desire not to lose their hold on the market. Thus there was an opportunity for the meat exporting company to carve out a market niche for itself.

When the sample batch of Chinese light globes arrived, they were of good quality and cost only 15 cents each to import (whereas the big companies were importing theirs for an average of 80 cents). So the deal was done. However, when the first shipment arrived, many of the lamps were faulty, or wrongly packaged, labelled or bar-coded. Two particular containers of them were satisfactory, and these formed the basis of the company's supply to the chain stores. Future imports by the company were arranged directly with the manufacturers of those particular globes.

On one of his trips to China, the former CEO saw the one-piece energy efficient lights (compact fluorescent globes) which were being sold in Hong Kong. He bought some and brought them home to Australia. However, once again there were problems with quality. Nevertheless, convinced that such globes had a future here, the company employed a design engineer to develop a better quality lamp, and succeeded in cornering the market here - 20% of the market in less than 3 months.

Fate once again played a hand, however, when a major international lighting manufacturer issued an injunction preventing the company from manufacturing the globes. The injunction was on the basis that the imported fluorescent tubes which formed part of the globes and which were manufactured in China were an infringement of the international manufacturer's patent. This stopped the company in their tracks. However, perhaps once again it was fate or serendipity, for it was at this point that the then CEO spoke to staff of the SECV, who advised that the future for compact fluorescent globes would be in two-piece globes rather than one-piece globes. The SECV stated that they had drawn up a new standard for compact fluorescent globes, which related to levels of power consumption and harmonic distortion.

This was seen by the company executives as a challenge, and they determined to be the first in the world to meet the new standard. However, despite having a post-graduate student working on the design problems for the next six months, nothing much seemed to happen. Then 'luck' or 'fate' again played a hand.

Through the door of a large multinational electronics company walked a man who said he knew how to overcome the power losses and harmonic distortion problems of two-piece compact fluorescent globes. His statement was "greeted with a stifled yawn", and he was told to bring back a working sample of his design for testing, and that if it passed the testing for a year, then the multinational company might be interested.

The man concerned was an avid reader, who had read of the problems confronting the two-piece lamp. He was also a pastor of a conservative Christian church. One day, as he walked past an electronics shop, he "received a vision". He went in and consulted an electronics catalogue, then went to the SECV to tell them that he knew how to solve the problems. The SECV sent him to this company, which signed an agreement with him that day. His invention now forms the basis of the two-piece globes the company manufactures.

This is not the only case of serendipity among the companies in this study. Another of the companies studied operates a distillery in which it ferments molasses to produce ethanol. For many years, the company had faced problems relating to the pollution caused by effluent from the distillery's operations. Although the solids component of the effluent was valuable as a potassium fertiliser, the dilute nature of the waste stream (with only 10% dissolved solids and 1% potassium content) meant that it was uneconomical to transport beyond 30 - 40 kilometres. The introduction of a new method of fermentation and distillation has resulted in the production of a more concentrated effluent which has the very balance of nutrients required to grow sugar cane in the soils in the area surrounding the distillery. What was once a waste disposal problem (costing hundreds of thousands of dollars to manage, and even then managing it ineffectively) has become a product for which demand now exceeds supply.

Several other executives highlighted issues associated with timing which could be considered (to an extent at least) to be 'serendipitous' in nature. For one company, the 'chance' coming together of the decline in 'local' supplies of crude oil, declining numbers of pre-1986 cars, and the government policy of phasing out lead in petrol by early next century, were helpful in that they prompted the upgrading of the company's refineries and placed the company in a strategically advantageous position to adopt more environmentally beneficial practices. For another company, it was simply the 'chance' connections made by the Chief Executive with other people with similar ideals which enabled him to establish the company successfully.

Australia's Culture of Innovation

In keeping with the literature (DITAC 1993; Lam undated; Ralston 1990), several companies have highlighted the importance for their success of the culture of innovation which they believe exists in Australia.

One executive of a large multinational corporation stated his belief that the youthfulness of Australia as a nation, and its multi-ethnic nature, have resulted in Australian people being relatively progressive. The willingness of Australian people and companies to 'pick up and run with' new ideas and inventions are seen as important factors in the success of this company. By contrast (according to the executive), the European subsidiaries of the corporation are in countries with longer traditions, where people and companies are slower to take on new ideas and technologies. The fact that the new range of 'green' products launched by the company was developed in Australia is (in the executive's view) a reflection of this innovative approach.

Similarly, an executive from an American-based company highlighted the importance of the culture of innovation in Australia (in comparison with the USA which, in the view of the executive, is much more conservative) in the local company's development of innovative approaches to environmental problems.

Access to Capital/Availability of Investment Funds

Access to capital is critical to the success of industry (Baden & Stroup 1991).

For the smaller locally-based companies in particular, access to capital through equity shareholders and/or investment funds has been an important factor contributing to their success. In one case, this capital was able to be secured from an 'ethical investment' company because of the 'green' nature of the manufacturing company.

Other External Factors

A range of other external factors have been identified which have assisted companies in this study to succeed as 'green' businesses.

The first is related to the policy context in which the companies are operating. Recent changes in policy, which have resulted in a move towards a user-pays basis for pricing of services such as water and electricity, have provided an economic incentive for householders to adopt more environmentally beneficial technologies relating to water and energy usage. This has therefore increased the market opportunity for such products.

The help obtained through positive publicity and feedback, both to the companies and to potential clients, concerning the benefits of companies' products has been acknowledged as an important factor in the success of a number of the companies studied. For example, the publicity received by one locally-based company from its participation in an industrial exhibition in Germany, has opened up the possibility of a number of options for expansion of the company's operations, including joint ventures and/or franchising. Another small locally-based company noted that, within one of its large client organisations, internal communication about the effectiveness of the company's product has resulted in additional sales of the product to other sections of the client organisation.

For one of the large overseas-based companies, three other external aids were identified. They were: the availability of access to up-to-date information through international conferences (which helps the company to keep up-to-date with developments by other companies and other countries); World Bank funding of development projects in developing nations (thereby creating a market for the company's products); and Australia's image as a 'green' country (which helps in the promotion of the company's products).

Another large overseas-based company highlighted the importance of the company's practice of 'bench marking' against ten other branches of the corporation around the world, which provides an incentive for environmental improvements. More objective worldwide bench marking which will result from the further development of environmental management standards by the International Standards Organisation (the ISO 14000 series) will, in the view of the company's environmental services manager, encourage ongoing improvements. Improvements in technology have also contributed to the successful 'greening' of the company.

Comparison of Literature and Case Study Data on Factors Assisting the 'Greening' of Companies

Just as the motivational factors identified through the case studies differed to some extent from those noted in the literature, so also the factors assisting companies did not directly correspond. This was true for both internal and external factors.

The findings of the case studies supported the literature concerning the importance of business skills and experience of management and senior staff. However, specific skills in networking, whilst highlighted as important in a number of the case studies, were not mentioned in the literature.

Several other internal factors which were not identified through the literature were noted by companies in this study. They were: features of the products being manufactured by the companies; prior activities of the organisation; availability of time for product development; and flexibility of manufacturing process.

Similarly, several additional external factors assisting companies were identified through the case studies. These were: government support in the form of grants, loans, etc.; the change to 'user pays' pricing for water and electricity; publicity and feedback; access to up-to-date information; the growth of markets in the developing world; Australia's image as a 'green' country; and the process of bench marking (including the development of international standards). In addition, the influence of 'serendipity' among the companies in this study appears to have been more important than the attention given to it in the literature would indicate.

Overview of the Findings on Factors Assisting Companies

A range of factors assisting companies to succeed as 'green' businesses has been identified through this study. These factors have been categorised as 'internal' - those which arise from within the companies themselves, and 'external' - those which impinge on companies from outside.

Almost two-thirds of the companies studied identified the skills and expertise of management and staff (an 'internal' factor) as critical to their success. The structure and functioning of companies was also seen as important, especially in terms of the capacity for effective decision-making. Commitment of key staff to environmental issues, which in several cases was linked to the culture of the 1960s and 1970s, was also critical. These three factors combined, cited by twenty-four of the thirty companies, provide the companies with the necessary technical and management skills to ensure success, and the leadership capacity to draw a commitment from the whole staff to improved environmental performance. In Giddens' terms they can be seen as 'authoritative resources'.

Internal access to 'allocative resources' in the form of capital was also acknowledged as an important influence on the success of companies, not simply in terms of their 'greening' but, for many smaller companies, in terms also of their survival. For some of the smaller companies, especially those which had been recently established, capital was not readily available 'internally', so their access to external sources of funds was critical. As indicated, this dependence on external sources of capital has been problematic for a number of the smaller companies.

Linkages with and/or support from other organisations were identified by almost half of the companies studied as important in their success. The linkages identified included those with industry associations, environmental regulators, government departments, semi-government instrumentalities and environmental groups. Interestingly, some of these linkages demonstrated an element of Giddens' 'duality of structure': for example, support from environmental groups has been both a medium for encouraging companies to adopt 'greener' processes/products, as well as an outcome of the adoption of such processes. Formal support from governments, for example in the form of grants and loans, was also identified as important, although the process of obtaining such support and the conditions governing such support undermine its overall value in some instances.

Product-related factors were also seen as important in the success of companies. Quality, price and the accuracy of claims made for the product/s in terms of their environmental impacts were all identified as contributing to the success or otherwise of the companies which manufacture them. The 'culture of innovation' in Australia was identified by several companies as fostering this product-related advantage, and the growing awareness of environmental issues in the community was seen as providing an expanding market for the expanding range of 'green' products.

As well as being motivating factors, environmental regulations and economic pressures have also been identified as factors which have assisted companies to succeed as 'green' businesses. In particular, stricter environmental regulations have provided market opportunity for companies which manufacture 'green' technology (for example, asbestos abatement equipment), and, together with economic pressures, have also encouraged companies to improve their environmental performance in order to reduce resource and waste disposal costs.

Perhaps the most unexpected finding of the study was the role of 'serendipity': the 'chance' coalescence of factors which (for several of the companies studied) was important in their success.

9   Hurdles and Hindrances - Factors Inhibiting the 'Greening' of Industry

What Hinders the 'Greening' of Companies?

There appears to be a subtle difference between what large companies mean by successful 'greening' of the company and hindrances to that success, and what those terms mean to small companies. In general, that relates to the fact that the focus of most small companies has been on the development of a 'green product', whereas the focus of most large companies has been on improving their own internal environmental management. However, these are generalisations, and exceptions to them can be found among the case study companies.

Fifteen different categories of factors hindering companies' success in their attempts to be 'green' manufacturers have been identified. Interestingly, there is considerable overlap between these factors and those identified as assisting the 'greening' of companies. Although some of the factors identified have elements which are inherent in the nature and/or structure of the companies themselves, most are related in some way at least to external factors. Hence they have not been divided into distinct categories of 'internal' and 'external' factors. The spread of the various factors across the study sample is depicted in Table 9.1. The categories are as follows:

- difficulty gaining access to finance/cash flow problems;
- variability in standards/regulations and their enforcement;
- limited size of local market;
- effects of recession;
- lack of support from environmental and consumer organisations;
- taxation arrangements;
- weaknesses of/absence of satisfactory environmental labelling scheme/monitoring of environmental claims;
- undermining of credibility of product/process by competitors;

- problems with government bureaucracy & conditions governing grants, contracts and government business development schemes;
- tariff policies;
- structure, size and profile of the companies & skills/experience of staff;
- community attitudes;
- cost of technology/product/process;
- cultural issues; and
- other.

Difficulty Gaining Access to Finance

One of the most common factors hindering the success of 'green' companies has been difficulty in gaining access to finance, either for capital works or to cover cash flow problems. This was mentioned as a problem by more than half of the companies studied, and confirms the findings of the literature review (Baden & Stroup 1991; McKinsey 1993; The Age Editorial 17 June 1993).

As one CEO put it: "there is no such thing as venture capital in Australia". This lack of access to start-up capital was noted as a major problem, especially for small companies which do not have the collateral to adequately secure large bank loans. For other companies the problem lies in the lack of access to funds for expansion.

Despite the banning of disposal of fluorescent tubes in landfill sites in both Europe and the USA, the company which manufactures the machine for disposal of fluorescent tubes has been unable to expand its sales into those potential markets due to lack of funds. The CEO noted that to establish the necessary marketing program would cost $250,000, a sum which is beyond the means of the company at this stage.

According to one of the other highly successful small local companies, this is a 'Catch 22' situation: companies cannot fulfil their potential without expanding into overseas markets, but they cannot expand into overseas markets because of lack of finance (which would be the outcome of such an expansion)! Furthermore, the need for funds occurs at the very time when companies have limited capacity to provide security for the funds. Once they can provide security, they are no longer at the point of needing funds.

Table 9.1:   Factors Hindering the 'Greening' of Industry

Factors ↓ / Company number →	1	2	3	4	5	6	7	8	9	10	11	12	13	14	15	16	17	18	19	20	21	22	23	24	25	26	27	28	29	30
Difficulty gaining access to capital/cash flow problems						✓	✓	✓	✓	✓	✓	✓	✓	✓															✓	✓
Variability in standards/regulations & their enforcement						✓	✓	✓	✓		✓	✓	✓	✓			✓								✓					
Limited size of local market	✓											✓	✓																	
Effects of recession						✓	✓	✓			✓	✓	✓				✓				✓			✓	✓			✓	✓	
Lack of support from environmental & consumer organis'ns							✓										✓				✓			✓	✓					
Taxation arrangements	✓																✓				✓				✓					
Lack of satisfactory. environmental labelling scheme	✓												✓																	

Undermining of credibility by competitors

Problems with gov't bureaucracy & grant conditions

Tariff policies

Structure, size & profile of co./skills & experience of staff

Community attitudes

Cost of technology/product/ process

Cultural issues

Other

Criticism of banks was widespread among the smaller companies in this study. One CEO commented that banks "only lend money to people who don't need it". Another expressed the view that banks and bank managers are generally "financially illiterate". He asserted that they do not have the skills to identify opportunities, and that the Tricontinental saga[1] has exacerbated this situation by bringing about a siege mentality within banks (a view which was also expressed by other study participants). Examples abound. One small company which wanted to borrow money to develop a prototype electric bicycle was refused by a 'development' bank on the basis that it was not the type of venture they normally lend for - the normal recipients of funds being corner stores and the like.

For one company the lack of available capital and the attitude of banks proved such a major problem that after six years in business, during which time the company had established itself in Victoria and was on the brink of establishing lucrative interstate and overseas markets, the company has been forced into liquidation. In the view of the CEO, the requirement by banks that "when you want to borrow $50, you have to give them $100 of bricks and mortar security" is the biggest problem that any business is facing today. The company experienced considerable difficulty in gaining lease finance for specialised equipment. He related the following story to illustrate the point:

> Going back to the time when I started to set up this plant, I approached a particular bank and asked them for lease finance. They said 'fine'. What the bank suggested was that we would just order the various machines from the manufacturers and get them to send the invoices to the bank, which would then pay the manufacturers. I pointed out to the bank that that was not going to happen in our instance because we had designed and developed the machinery ourselves and we had to build it. The bank's attitude was 'well, we really can't do a lease on something that's not in existence - you have to have a physical, tangible asset that the leasing company can take a charge on'.

---

[1]Tricontinental was the merchant banking arm of the State Bank of Victoria, which collapsed in 1990 with losses of around $2 billion. The collapse was the result of the failure of a number of companies which had obtained venture finance through the bank. (Armstrong & Gross, 1995 p. 302)

So I said 'well what do we do now?' and they said 'well, it doesn't matter; just give us the title to your property and we'll advance you the funds on the property, and you can go ahead and build your machines. Once the machines are physically in existence, we'll then do the 25 year lease on the machines, and that pays out the mortgage on your property'. So we got to the stage where we had the machines 95% completed and in fact we were at the point where we were looking for the final stages to be put in place. In particular there was a $54,000 bill for the wiring - to do the electrical switchboards and so on. Anyway, I went back to the bank and said 'Right we're just about ready to commission the plant. Can you get your leasing company to come out? So they sent their leasing company out and the net result of that was that the leasing company said: 'Beautiful looking machinery, but we're a bit worried about the economy. Interest rates are going to go through the roof and we think there's a recession coming - we don't want to know about it'. At that stage I'd spent over $800,000 and thirteen months time, and the leasing company said 'the machinery's too specialised. It's not like a Mercedes Benz car where if anything happens we can grab it and sell it'.

So I went back to the bank and asked 'what do we do now? The bank said 'it's a bit of a problem, but what the leasing company has said is correct - there is a recession coming and interest rates are going through the roof. So what we'll do is that we'll leave it where it is. We're happy with the security on the title of the property, and it will be at cheaper interest than leasing because it's commercial bills'. So I said 'Well I don't mind'. Then came the crunch: I said 'well I'm going to need another $54,000 to do the electrical wiring, and I reckon I'll need about $200,000 to start with stock and working capital'. 'Oh we can't give you any more' (said the bank). I said 'what do you mean you can't give me any more? There's $800,000 been spent and I need $54,000 to put the electrical work in and I need a couple of hundred thousand for working capital'. 'Oh well (said the bank), we can only lend to 50% of the value of your property, and that's already full bore'. I said 'Hang on - this was a temporary situation: when I came to you thirteen months ago, the agreement was you'd write a 25 year lease on my plant which was going to cost a million dollars. As it's turned out we've built it for just under $800,000'. 'Oh sorry' was the bank's response.

In desperation, the CEO approached another bank - one which was supposedly more business development oriented. He ultimately obtained a loan of $250,000 and the business began operation.

All went well for a few years during which the loan for $250,000 was reduced to $50,000, the pet litter manufacturing business was established and expanded market opportunities were identified and negotiated (including interstate and overseas markets), with firm orders Australia-wide which indicated a likely three- or four-fold increase in revenue, resulting in profits of around $100,000 per month. Negotiations with potential buyers in Japan indicated a likelihood of a $3-$5 million market annually.

In anticipation of the need for increased levels of production, the company moved to new premises in May 1995. However, a major problem with the electricity supply to the new premises emerged. Having been advised by the electricity company that it would take six to eight months to upgrade the power supply, the CEO was forced to buy a diesel generator to cover the shortfall in power supply. The generator purchased (second hand) by the company turned out to be faulty, and a few weeks elapsed before full production could be resumed. Despite cash flow problems in April, May and June of 1995 as a result of moving premises and the subsequent delay in returning to full production, the company still managed to make its regular payments to the bank to reduce the loan. However, another problem emerged with the diesel motor, and on the basis of expert advice, the CEO decided to totally rebuild the generator at a cost of an extra $15,000 (on top of what had already been spent). So he went to the bank to ask for an extension of the company's overdraft facility from $10,000 to $25,000 to enable the repairs to be undertaken. The CEO was told that he would have an answer to his request within a few days.

In the meantime, payments from supermarkets for past supplies of pet litter were received and banked, and the CEO assumed that his existing overdraft arrangements with the bank would continue until such time as new arrangements had been agreed. However, a few days later, when he went to draw money to pay staff, he was informed that the company's $10,000 overdraft facility had been withdrawn. He was unable to pay his staff, and (having no money to undertake the repairs to the generator) was unable to get back into production. By this stage it was early August, and the company (because of its problems with the power supply, resulting in a halt to production) had missed its July and August loan repayments of $5,000 each. Within a matter of days, the bank foreclosed on the loan.

To avoid losing the business, the CEO sought people to invest in the business in return for a share in the company. He managed to identify two potential investors who were willing to put sufficient capital into the company to pay out the bank in full, subject to the transfer of the lease to the new company name, and an offer in writing to this effect was submitted to the bank. The landlord was a semi-government instrumentality and the new investors had been advised that the transfer of the lease would take between two and three weeks to effect. However, the bank went ahead with the foreclosure, the manager asserting that the lease transfer was more likely to take three months than three weeks, and that that was too long.

Having spent a total of $1.7 million on the business, the CEO lost it all for the sake of a $100,000 debt - the $50,000 loan (which was not actually due for repayment) plus two months of accrued interest, plus additional sundry debts resulting from the discontinuation of the business. The former CEO's anger and frustration are summed up in his statement that he "would never ever trust a bank again". Twice (once with the first bank defaulting on the lease agreement, and once with the second bank closing the file on the loan) he had suffered at the hands of banks. In his view, the deregulation of banking has been a major problem, with banks becoming "a law unto themselves". When he asked the bank manager why the bank was foreclosing on the loan, the bank manager said:

It costs us more money to administer the balance of the debt. If you owed us a quarter of a million dollars, then we'd probably keep going.

Asked why the bank would not allow the company to trade its way out of its difficulties, the bank manager said:

We can't lodge an insurance claim unless we go through the legal process of winding you up.

Another example of problems with obtaining finance through banks comes from one of the (now) large overseas-based companies. However, in this case the problems were overcome, resulting in the successful establishment and expansion of the company.

The founder and her husband owned a small hotel in the south of England, and she assumed that, using the hotel as collateral, she would have no difficulty in obtaining finance from the bank to start the business.

But, as her autobiography points out, it was not so simple. The attitude of banks to lending (at least in the 1970s) was discriminatory, disadvantaging women and people who present themselves or their potential businesses in an 'alternative' style.

> Unfortunately, I went about it in entirely the wrong way. I made an appointment to see the bank manager and turned up wearing a Bob Dylan T-shirt with Samantha on my hip and Justine clinging to my jeans. It just did not occur to me that I should be anything other than my normal self. I was enthusiastic and I gabbled on about my great idea, flinging out all this information about how I had discovered these natural ingredients when I was travelling, and I'd got this great name, ..., and all I needed was £4,000 to get started. I got quite carried away in my excitement, but I was on my own. I discovered that you don't go to a bank manager with enthusiasm - that is the last thing he cares about. When I had finished, he leaned back in his chair and said that he wasn't going to lend me any money because we were too much in debt already. I was stunned.
>
> I went home to Gordon absolutely crushed. 'That's it,' I said. 'It's hopeless. The bank won't give me any money.' I was ready to give up, but Gordon is much more tenacious than I am. 'We will get the money,' he said, 'But we are going to have to play them at their own game.' He told me to go out and buy a business suit, and got an accountant friend to draw up an impressive-looking 'business plan', with projected profit and loss figures and a lot of gobbledegook, all bound in a plastic folder.
>
> A week later we went back to the same bank for an interview with the same manager. This time I left the children behind and Gordon came with me. We were both dressed in suits. Gordon handed over our little presentation, the bank manager flipped through it for a couple of minutes and then authorised a loan of £4,000, just like that, using the hotel as collateral. I was relieved - but I was angry, too, that I had been turned down the first time. After all, I was the same person with the same idea. It was clear to me that bank managers did not want to deal with mothers with babies. When we went back the second time I might just as well not have been there, because the manager only talked to Gordon anyway. I was cast in the role of the little woman who just happened to be along.

Reflecting on this experience in her autobiography, the founder goes on to say:

I often wonder how many fantastic ideas never came to fruition because of the lack of imagination of those people who sit behind desks in banks all over the country and who are too frightened to take a gamble. There are only two ways of raising money: the hard way and the very hard way!

Variability in Standards/Regulations and their Enforcement

Another major hindrance to the 'greening' of companies (noted by one-third of the companies in the study) is the lack of consistency in environmental standards and regulations and their enforcement (Baden & Stroup 1991; Commission of the European Communities 1992; Eckersley 1995; Elkington 1987; Marsh 1991). Among the smaller companies in this study, there is a belief that lack of consistency in standards across Australia limits the market for 'green' products.

An example of the lack of consistency in standards and regulations is outlined in this extract from a letter written by the former CEO of the company which manufactures two-part compact fluorescent light globes:

> As an Australian manufacturer of a second generation high technology Compact Fluorescent Lamp (we) must comply with extremely stringent Australian Standard AS3134.
>
> With one exception no other manufacturer in the world can meet the safety and electrical disturbance limits contained in ... AS3134.
>
> Importers such as ... cannot meet the Australian Standard. However, because one piece Compact Fluorescent Lamps are classified as ordinary globes, ... (they) do not presently have to pass any Australian Standard, much less AS3134.
>
> Australia is the only country in the world that does not subject all Compact Fluorescent Lamps to an identical Government standard.

Such a requirement (for the Australian manufacturer to meet the Standard) results in additional costs of approximately $4 per globe - in effect, a de facto tariff protecting imported products against local products.

Another company, which manufactures a laundry detergent which contains no petrochemicals or phosphates, drew attention to the failure by the Trade Practices Commission to enforce guidelines relating to environmental claims for marketing. As a result (according to the CEO), companies whose claims for their products have not been verified are allowed to continue to make dubious environmental claims for their products and thereby gain an unfair advantage over companies which conform to the guidelines. In addition, the CEO drew attention to the failure of the Australian Standards Association to complete its review of the standards for biodegradability of detergent surfactants - a review which has been in progress for more than six years. In the view of the CEO, the resulting inadequate standards (which are outdated by comparison with those established by the International Standards Organisation) allow companies which are not meeting the necessary standards (ISO) to still claim that they are meeting the standard for biodegradability.

The companies which noted problems due to lack of consistency in standards and their enforcement were not limited to the small local companies. Several of the large multinational companies also drew attention to this problem. One noted that lack of uniformity of regulations for trade wastes throughout Australasia hinders the adoption of a corporate approach to waste management.

An executive of another large multinational company noted that there is scepticism about the power of the EPA which undermines its effectiveness as a regulatory body. This has resulted in some industry executives (including some in his company) being cynical about the effectiveness of the EPA. The executive said:

> They know that not too many people have been gaoled; they know that America is a different world in terms of litigation. So therefore they get cynical, and say 'I know I'm not environmentally under control but I'm not being picked up on it, so I'm willing to take the risk'.

This scepticism is compounded by a lack of trust in the EPA which relates to the inconsistency in approach by the EPA. Referring to a threatened EPA waste minimisation study, which ultimately became a company-based cleaner production program, the executive stated:

> It went from a massive threat - ' we're going to go through you like a dose of salts' - to one man from the EPA having very small input.

The lack of trust also relates to role conflict between the regulatory role of the EPA and its advisory role, which makes companies suspicious about the motives for EPA staff offering to come in to companies and give advice.

One of the smaller locally-based companies, which manufactures and markets erosion control and revegetation products, supported the view that 'green' industry is inhibited by lack of consistency in regulation. Its CEO expressed the view that the regulations in Victoria relating to erosion and consequent siltation of waterways are "antiquated". He compared New South Wales, where "you can't dump a truckload of soil on your nature strip without putting in some sort of protection to stop that silt getting into the drainage system" with the huge amount of silt lost through runoff at the South Eastern Arterial construction site at the junction with Warrigal Road.[2] Lack of enforcement of regulations is also, in the opinion of the CEO, a problem. He sees this as the result of a combination of factors: the EPA is part of the bureaucracy and (in his words) "works office hours", so its inspectors are not necessarily around when the damage is being done (eg. after hours, or on weekends). He also believes that the EPA lacks funds (a view expressed by executives of several other companies as well), and is subject to pressure from politicians who don't want to upset the construction companies and perhaps threaten jobs.

Limited Size of Local Market

The limitations posed by the small size of the domestic market in Australia which were noted in the literature review (Australian Manufacturing Council 1994; McKinsey 1993; Saddler 1990) have been confirmed by several of the companies studied.

An executive from one small local company which manufactures electric bicycles noted several impacts resulting from this. The first was the restricted number of forward orders for the product, making the business less attractive for potential investors. The second was the higher component costs (and thus the higher overall cost for the product) due to lack of economies of scale.

Similar views were expressed by the CEO of a locally-based company which manufactures fluidised bed furnaces for the heat treatment of metals. He pointed out that the limited size of the Australian market is a serious problem for companies such as his, especially given the specialised nature of the products, since it reduces the opportunity for economies of scale. Where export opportunities for products are found, they may be specialised

---

[2]The junction of the South-Eastern Arterial and Warrigal Road is situated in the south-eastern suburbs of Melbourne.

applications of Australian technology. As a result, companies such as this are constantly faced with the task of developing new one-off applications of their technology, and undertaking that development at a distance from the situation in which it will be used. These factors place Australian companies at a disadvantage in comparison with their overseas competitors who have local opportunities for product development and modification and large markets offering economies of scale in production.

Effects of Recession

Although not mentioned in the literature, one of the most commonly identified hindrances to the success of 'green' companies in Australia (mentioned by almost half of all companies studied) was the recession. According to study participants, this hindrance occurred in several ways. First, it drew the community's attention away from environmental concerns towards economic concerns, and thereby reduced the consumer market for 'green' products. Secondly, it discouraged companies from spending the money required to adopt new 'greener' technologies, which both reduced the 'greening' of companies and reduced the market for 'green' industrial products.

For example, the former CEO of the company which manufactured home insulation from waste paper commented that the economic downturn over recent years had a negative impact on the company. He identified two main groups of people: "there are those that just don't have any money, and there are those that have the money but are too frightened to spend it". He stated that the optional nature of insulation as a product (at least in relation to existing properties) has meant that even those who have money have been reluctant to spend it on insulation in case they find themselves unemployed in the future and need their capital resources to live on. In addition, he noted that the building industry has also gone through a downturn, which has resulted in less home building and a consequent reduction in the market for insulation.

Similar comments were made by a range of companies including both smaller local companies and large overseas-based companies: that the recession had resulted in the reduction in the size of the market for 'green' products and the contraction of companies' own spending on environmental improvements.

One company identified a quite different (although indirectly related) impact of the recession: that the recession has resulted in people feeling uncertain about entering fields of education related to manufacturing (preferring instead to become doctors and lawyers), with the result that this company has experienced difficulty in obtaining suitably qualified engineers locally, and is having to look overseas for staff.

Lack of Support, or Opposition, from Environmentalists, Consumer Organisations and Other Stakeholders

The support from environmentalists referred to in the literature (Elkington 1987; Leighton 1992; Marsh 1991) as important in changing corporate behaviour towards the environment has been inadequate, according to seven of the companies in this study. The same applies in many cases to consumer organisations and other key stakeholders.

The problems in relationships between companies and environmental/consumer organisations and other stakeholders ranged from simply "lack of support from environmental and consumer organisations" highlighted by one small locally-based company, through to outright opposition cited by several others.

One small local company which manufactures ultraviolet radiation monitors indicated that lack of support from the Anti-Cancer Council was a major stumbling block to the success of both the electronic and the card versions of the monitor. The Director of the Council expressed the view (quite rightly, in the view of the products' inventor) that there is no safe level of ultra-violet radiation. The Council therefore takes the view that levels of UV radiation should not be monitored because that would infer that there is a safe level. According to the inventor, the Council believes that any indication (for example, on a public display monitor or on a card) which infers that the UV level might be safe leaves the authority in charge of the display open to litigation in the event of skin cancer developing. This lack of support removed a major potential marketing opportunity for the company, and has resulted in the company having very limited success. In the words of the inventor, as an ultra violet radiation monitoring equipment organisation, its "pulse is weak".

Another company, which manufactures equipment designed to remove asbestos from pipes, vessels and valves etc. safely while 'on line', was hindered in its initial phases by opposition from trade unions (which were concerned because the process is less labour intensive than other methods of asbestos abatement, and might therefore result in a reduction in employment) and from occupational hygienists (who were opposed to the process because it reduced the need for monitoring, which is their livelihood). These problems have since been largely overcome, but they did hinder the company in its establishment phase.

Opposition from an environmental organisation was also experienced by the developer of a machine for the direct seeding of trees. According to the inventor, a major environmental organisation involved in tree planting 'white-anted' the reputation of the machine in the major commercial markets available to the company: mining and forestry companies. This opposition made it difficult for the company to provide potential buyers with referees who could show them large-scale examples of plantations developed using the machine. (Interestingly, an urban arm of the environmental organisation began negotiations with the company to purchase one of the machines. They sent people to visit the inventor and see the machine and how it worked. They took photographs and took measurements of the machine. After about eight months, when asked by the inventor what they wanted to do about it and when they wanted the machine, it emerged that they had commissioned someone to make a machine for them, having obtained the design and measurements from the inventor.)

Taxation Arrangements

Several companies in this study drew attention to the difficulties caused for them by the existing taxation system in Australia. The literature identifies taxation as an issue affecting the 'greening' of industry (Committee for Economic Development of Australia 1992; Dabner 1991; Hawken 1993; Schmidheiny 1992). However, whereas the literature focuses broadly on the distortion of the market through taxation arrangements, the issues raised by the companies in this study are more narrowly focused.

One small locally-based company highlighted the difficulties posed by taxation policies which require the company to pay the sales tax on its products before it has received payment from retailers for the products it has supplied.

Another small company (which manufactures biological remediation systems for air and soil pollution) pointed out that the nature of the taxation system compounds cash flow problems experienced by small, developing companies which have large peaks and troughs in income because of the nature of their products. The CEO stated that in a company such as his, while several million dollars may be earned in one financial year, there may be no profit at all in the subsequent year or two. Yet the income earned is taxed as if it was to be repeated in the following years. As a result, there is limited opportunity for the company to reinvest the profits in the business and thereby to build the business to the point where the peaks and troughs in cash flow and staffing levels are evened out.

Absence of Satisfactory Environmental Labelling Scheme/Monitoring of Environmental Claims

Given the concerns expressed in the literature about the inadequacy of environmental labelling schemes and the monitoring of environmental claims (MacKenzie 1991; Schumpeter 1992; West 1995), it is not surprising that three of the companies in this study have highlighted this as a hindrance to their success.

The CEO of one small local company which was part of the Environmental Choice program stated that the shortcomings of that program had been a major cause of difficulties for the company. He indicated that the company supports the concept of an independent environmental claims evaluation. The CEO believes that such an evaluation is important for the protection of consumers and of companies which are genuinely wanting to make improvements in terms of reducing their environmental impact. However, he believes that the failure of the program to make any value judgements about products has meant that companies which paid the fees and had their environmental claims verified have received little advantage. Any advantage which was received - the right to use the 'Environmental Choice' symbol on their products - became (in the view of the CEO) a disadvantage in the light of widely publicised criticisms of the Environmental Choice program by environmental, consumer and industry groups. He says:

> we were part of it, and although individually I don't think that anybody has been able to fault our product in terms of what we say about our product and what we're doing with the product, however we were guilty by association, I guess. I guess to that extent, environmental organisations probably haven't given our product very much credibility. ... So rather than helping us it probably hindered us.

For one of the large overseas-based companies, the Environmental Choice program proved at best no advantage. Research by the company in 1993 found that consumers were seriously concerned about the environment, and that they were receiving confusing messages relating to environmental effects of products. They expressed a strong desire for independent assessment of products, and the CSIRO was the choice of 80% of consumers as the appropriate independent assessment authority. Although the company's products had been assessed by Environmental Choice, this was meaningless to the majority of consumers as they had never heard of the program.

Another of the small locally-based companies pointed out that the 'Environmental Choice' program was too expensive and was therefore limited in its accessibility for small companies. This reinforced the existing advantage which large (often multi-national) companies have over small local companies.

Undermining of Credibility of Product/Process by Competitors

Although not mentioned at all in the literature, a factor hindering the success of four of the companies in this study was the undermining of the credibility of their product or process by competitors. This occurs at several different levels.

For example, the company which manufactures bio-remediation systems for air and soil pollution has been hampered by what the CEO described as "the harsh realities of the marketplace". This has included companies which offer competing technologies making environmental claims for their products which (in the view of the CEO) are not justified, and disinformation about bio-filtration systems - claims by competitors that biological remediation techniques are slow and ineffective. As a result of this, 70% of potential contracts for the company are lost.

Another company - the manufacturer of house insulation from waste paper - drew attention to the indirect effect on companies such as his from the undermining of the credibility of the whole insulation industry by 'cowboys' who do not adhere to standards.

Like the company which developed the tree planting machine, the CEO of another company, which manufactures a specialised lubrication product, claims that his company has suffered "commercial sabotage". He states that the credibility of his company's product has been undermined by oil companies spreading misleading information about the company's product, motivated by the impact that the product could have on the sales of fuel and oil.

The company which manufactures the equipment for removal of asbestos also suffered similar problems, with competitors 'bad-mouthing' the process and suggesting that it does not work.

Problems with Government Bureaucracy and Conditions Governing Grants, Contracts and Government-funded Business Development Schemes

Difficulties in dealing with government bureaucracies, and the related difficulties resulting from the conditions governing grants, contracts and government-funded business development schemes are, according to both the literature and the case study data, another major source of hindrance to 'green' companies (Magazanik 1993; McKinsey 1993).

One small company studied highlighted the problems relating to government tendering processes. The CEO stated that, in most cases, companies tendering for government contracts are required to have quality assurance accreditation in accordance with ISO 9000. To obtain such accreditation initially took around 18 months and cost between $50,000 and $60,000. Recent initiatives have seen this cost reduced to $15,000, but a significant time input by company personnel is still required. For small companies, to expend both the time and the money necessary to obtain such accreditation is out of the question, and they are therefore excluded from government contracts. Small companies are also disadvantaged by other government criteria for assessing tenders for government contracts - criteria relating to turnover, profit etc., which advantage big companies at the expense of small firms.

The CEO of another company stated that in addition to the bureaucracy and form-filling in which small businesses find themselves 'engulfed', companies such as his also experience difficulties because of inappropriate grant application conditions. For example, he noted that R & D grants from the government require a minimum expenditure of $30,000 per annum - a condition not appropriate for a small company such as his where the R & D is spread over time. Similarly, government export grants exempt the first $15,000 of expenditure - a large sum to a small company such as his. Thus government support schemes are geared to help larger companies (which often have a greater capacity to obtain finance anyway) rather than small companies (which do not).

One small local manufacturer drew attention to the difficulties which his company had experienced because of the failure of the Federal Government to release funds granted to the company through Austrade as an Export Market Development Grant. The payment was withheld for over a year, due to a technicality. This forced the company to limit its activities. In the view of the CEO, this failure to release the funds relates to what he describes as "an attitude of scarcity instead of abundance among public servants". In his view, the government workers believe that they have to protect the 'government's' money, instead of seeing that if they approve the funding, the corporate sector will be able to make more money for the country. There is (in his view) an attitude among public servants of keeping to an absolute minimum the amount of money given away by the government.

Several CEOs expressed the view that organisations such as the Small Business Development Corporation do not provide the support for small businesses which is needed. One stated that government grants to small business are too small (at $5,000 - $10,000) to be effective, and are more a political move than a serious attempt to assist small business. In his view, schemes such as the Victorian Economic Development Corporation (VEDC)[3] were (in themselves) good. The only problem was that the wrong people were put in charge of administering the schemes - people who lacked the ability to assess the likely success of proposed ventures. His company (which has been highly successful) approached the VEDC for funds but was rejected. Other companies which gained funds from the VEDC have collapsed.

Other companies confirm the fact that there are difficulties associated with government grant and business development schemes. One study participant commented that the tendency of governments to charge for services provided by Austrade makes it difficult for small companies to access the benefits of association with such organisations, because of needing to pay large sums of money 'up-front'. One rurally-located company had difficulty even identifying appropriate sources of advice and support. In addition, the specialised agricultural arm of Austrade known as

---

[3]The VEDC was set up by the Victorian Government in 1981 to "facilitate and encourage the development of Victorian industry" (Report of Inquiry: Victorian Economic Development Corporation 1989 p. 3), but by late 1988 it had become "in a commercial sense, insolvent" (ibid p. 4).

Agrotech, with which companies manufacturing agricultural products would be dealing, has as its directors people from companies which are direct competitors of the applicant company. Companies are loath to apply for assistance because they would be required to disclose to those directors sensitive details of the company which they would not otherwise disclose to their competitors.

In the view of one respondent (a view developed as a result of his experience in dealing with government departments and organisations such as Austrade) a major problem in dealing with such bodies is that they are often less interested in the value of the technology or the project than they are in the political kudos they will gain from the publicity associated with it.

A further problem highlighted by another company was the system of accounting within government that limits the thinking of sections and departments to their narrow domain, instead of encouraging a broader view. The company's CEO approached the vehicle maintenance section of a government instrumentality which has a large fleet of vehicles, suggesting that they could benefit from the company's product creating more efficiency in fuel consumption. He was told that the maintenance section does not have anything to do with fuel economy, so they do not worry about it - that is the domain of another section. Referred to that other section, the CEO was told that the fleet was already operating within budget, so there was no need to do anything to improve efficiency.

Another example of problems associated with government accounting procedures was provided by the CEO of the company which manufactures erosion control and revegetation products. He cited the case of a major road development for which he had quoted a cost of $8,000 - $10,000 to treat the batters to prevent erosion. Because the project was running close to budget, he was told that the money for additional capital works (which would prevent any erosion) could not be justified, but that there would be $5,000 each quarter (in the maintenance budget) available for repairing the damage caused by erosion.

In some cases, it is not just apathy but active opposition which companies receive from government bureaucracies. According to the inventor of the direct tree seeding machine, scepticism and resistance from the bureaucracy, resulting from what he believes to be the bureaucracy's desire to control the whole area of farm tree planting, has undermined acceptance of the concept and technology of direct tree seeding.

Tariff Policies

Although only obliquely referred to in the literature (McKinsey 1993), trade and tariff policies have been noted as a significant hindrance to several companies in this study.

According to the CEO of a fabric dyeing company, government policies of reducing tariffs and quotas, and allowing an increase in cheap imports, have undermined the success of the whole textile, clothing and footwear industry, including his company. Similar effects have been felt by the automobile manufacturing company in this study, as a result of the lowering of tariffs against imports.

For one company in the study (a chemical manufacturer), the effect of changing tariff arrangements is twofold: it undermines the viability of the company in Australia, and it threatens the ability of the Australian company to secure investment by its parent company in new technology here. That will, in the view of the informant, ultimately affect the profitability of the Australian company and its ability to adopt more environmentally sound management practices.

Structure, Size and Profile of the Company, and Skills/Experience of Staff

The literature highlights a number of aspects inherent in companies which hinder their success as 'green' businesses, focusing mainly on lack of skills and/or experience in management (Coyne 1993; McKinsey 1993; Pappas et al. 1990). This study confirms that view, and draws attention to a number of other aspects of companies which have hindered their success.

Lack of a recognised company 'profile' has been cited by three of the companies as a significant hindrance to their success. One small company which sells its products on the export market indicated that being what the CEO called "a no name company" - that is, not having an established brand name - impedes the company to some extent in its competition with comparable products manufactured by well-known American companies. This view was also expressed by the CEO of another small company which manufactures bio-remediation systems for air and soil pollution. He stated that when companies spend a large sum of money on purchasing a product, they expect to be dealing with a high profile company. In his view, small companies such as this, which do not operate out of large, plush offices, and which do not have large budgets for marketing and promotion, have difficulty establishing their credibility with potential purchasers.

The same CEO drew attention to another disadvantage he believes affects small companies: lack of total quality management practices. He believes that managers in small companies may become isolated, and are not questioned enough, because the companies do not have within them people with the knowledge base to challenge the management. In big companies, this questioning helps to stop management making mistakes. According to the CEO, this is a disadvantage in that although "I can be totally responsible for the decisions made, I am also totally responsible for the stuff-ups!"

Lack of management skills and experience was one of several 'internal' problems hindering the success of another small local company. Unlike the CEOs of many companies, the interviewee came from a working class background, and had no background in financial management. The driving force in establishing this company was his spiritually-based commitment to the welfare of humanity and the environment, and that has influenced the directions taken by the company. That has meant in some cases that the company has been to some extent running a crusade to change the attitudes of people to the environment at the same time as it has been attempting to establish itself commercially. In the view of the CEO, this may have made the task more difficult than necessary. It may have been better to establish the company on a firm commercial footing, and then use its commercial strength to influence community attitudes. In addition, because the company does not physically manufacture the product itself, but contracts out the blending of the product to another company, problems have been experienced in relation to quality control and lack of commitment by the sub-contractor's workers. Those problems appear to have been overcome by a change of sub-contractor, but the potential for problems with sub-contractors remains an issue for the company because sub-contractors do not have the same commitment to humanity and the environment.

Two other small local companies drew attention to another 'internal' problem: that of competing demands and pressures. For example, the inventor of the direct tree seeding machine noted that within the company itself, a factor limiting the success of the product has been related to the size of the company. With only two partners, and given the wide range of other (competing) interests of the inventor and his wife - for example, he is a professional artist and runs a 4000 acre sheep station, as well as working as a consultant on revegetation - there is a limit to the amount of time and energy they have to put into marketing the machine.

'Internal' problems hindering the success of companies are not restricted, however, to the smaller local companies. An executive of a large overseas-based company stated that inevitable production pressures on-site (such as conflicting demands for the time and energy of staff) can sometimes mean that small environmental matters can be overlooked. Another of the large overseas-based companies indicated that successful promotion of the company's products as 'environmentally preferred' has been hampered by the limited size of the company's advertising budget. The national sales manager pointed out that a Japanese-based competitor has recently increased its advertising budget by more than the total budget for the Australian arm of this company.

Another large overseas-based company highlighted several other internal problems affecting its environmental performance. An internal environmental report prepared for the company in 1991 has drawn attention to difficulties relating to a lack of communication between the parent company and the Australian company on environmental issues. In addition, the report has highlighted the need for someone in the senior management of the Australian company to 'own' the environment as an issue. Although the company is 'successful' in business terms and significant achievements have been made by the company in terms of environmental protection, the environmental report has indicated that more could be achieved.

One of the large Australian companies indicated that whilst it has been highly successful in business terms, its success as a 'green' manufacturer has been limited by several internal factors. Within a company as large as this one, and with such diverse business operations, it is difficult (according to executives) to achieve consistent standards of environmental management. This is further compounded by the internationalisation of the company, which operates within a number of different legislative/regulatory frameworks and within a range of different environmental, social and cultural settings, involving different issues and expectations.

According to the executives interviewed, capacities for improved environmental management vary across the company's businesses. For example, the nature of the steel manufacturing subsidiary company's business, which is highly energy intensive and dependent on fossil fuels, places some constraints on the extent to which the company can improve the external perception of its environmental performance.

Another problem highlighted by the interviewees relates to community perceptions on the availability of 'clean' (as distinct from 'cleaner') technologies. They indicated concern at what they see as a prevalent mis-perception in the community that such technologies are available for every industrial process, and that so-called 'end of pipe solutions' are unnecessary. Such a 'black or white attitude' is seen as unhelpful in that it ignores the realities confronting most companies which often do not have access to clean technology, and even if they do, have to take into account the time scales within which such changes can be effected without undermining the stability of the company. For companies such as this which have huge capital investment in expensive equipment which has a relatively long life-span, the move to clean or even cleaner production is (in the opinion of the executives) more difficult than for a company with smaller capital investment.

Another factor which has hindered the environmental management of the company has been the fact that until five years ago, there was no section within the company responsible for environmental issues. Environmental professionals were located at the individual site level and dealt only with environmental issues relevant to the particular site. Therefore there was a lack of broad corporate environmental policy, as well as a lack of interface between the company and the government on environmental issues and policies which could impact on the company. This inhibited the ability of the company to understand the broad impact on the company of new national and international laws and treaties, and also the ability of the company to protect its own interests by feeding into the development of such policies, laws and treaties.

The diverse nature of the company's business operations, the variety of management structures in the individual businesses, and the vast geographic spread of the company's business locations, combine to make it difficult to co-ordinate an overall approach to the company's management including its environmental management. One difficulty in such a diverse organisation is the development of a mechanism to ensure that the information on environmental issues confronting each of the individual businesses is synthesised and developed into appropriate policies and procedures. The geographic spread of the company (which has worldwide operations) creates difficulties relating to the variety of regulations applying in the different legal jurisdictions.

Another large overseas-based chemical company drew attention to three 'internal' factors which have hindered its success as a 'green' business:

joint venture arrangements; company history; and company size. Joint ventures with other companies make it difficult in some cases to enforce the company's own high environmental standards. This is particularly difficult where the company is not the majority shareholder in the partnership. The history of the company is also a hindrance in terms of the emotional baggage that the company carries as a result of its activities in the 1960s and 1970s. The interviewee indicated that that is still raised as an issue in public meetings, and still clearly affects the image of the company. In Australia, the decline in the size of the company over recent years has meant that there is a problem in terms of 'critical mass'. This has occurred at the same time as the organisation has been expanding elsewhere, which means that there has been a reduction in the ability of the Australian company to influence company policy internationally.

Community Attitudes

Although there is evidence within the literature of the positive influence of community attitudes, there do not appear to be any references to community scepticism and lack of awareness as hindrances to the 'greening' of industry. Nevertheless, this was among the more common 'hindrances' identified through the case studies, being identified by almost half of the companies studied.

Several small companies drew attention to a lack of community awareness of environmental issues in general (and to issues relevant to their companies in particular) as a hindrance to their companies' success. For example, the designer of the polluted water separator stated that, in his opinion, the unwillingness of relevant authorities to acknowledge the problem of water pollution has resulted in a lack of awareness of the problem in the community, and therefore has limited the potential market for his product. Similarly, the CEO of the fabric dyeing company suggested that a major hindrance to its business had been lack of awareness or concern in the community about the environmental issues associated with the manufacturing of goods they purchase.

The CEO of the company which manufactures erosion control and revegetation products drew attention particularly to differences in levels of environmental awareness around Australia. In his view, lack of awareness of erosion as an environmental problem has inhibited the company's success. He related the story of attending a 'Landcare' conference at

Wangaratta[4] and seeing an example of soil erosion in a creek bed where 300 m^2 of topsoil had been removed (washed away) in a week. He said:

> If I was the next door neighbour of that farmer and went on to his property with a truck and a tractor and removed 300m^2 of topsoil, he'd get his gun out and shoot me!

The CEO described erosion as a "silent thief". He compared this lack of awareness in Victoria with the recent growth in awareness in New South Wales, which has much tougher legislation. Attending an engineering field day in New South Wales each of the last three years, he has found that attitudes to erosion control products have moved from "Erosion? Oh yeah I've thought about that, but no, I'm not really interested." to "Erosion control! We need that."

One of the major hindrances affecting the company which manufactures bio-remediation systems for air and soil pollution has been a lack of understanding, both within industry and in the community at large, of the possibilities offered by biological remediation systems.

For other companies, it has not just been apathy or lack of understanding but also scepticism which has inhibited their success as 'green' businesses. The company which manufactures the specialised lubrication product has had to overcome both apathy about the environment, and disbelief in the product itself and in the motives of the company. That disbelief has been fuelled by the existence on the market of a number of oil-additives which are said to be effective in reducing engine friction but which, in fact, are ineffective. This has resulted in scepticism towards the company and its product.

An executive of the company which manufactures solar energy equipment highlighted several problems relating to community acceptance of solar technology. He stated that the long lead time in the development of new solar technologies from the ideas stage to the production stage is a problem for the industry, especially when publicity is given to the concept at an early stage. The lack of people with the skills and knowledge necessary to install and maintain solar systems further undermines community acceptance of the technology.

For another company (the manufacturer of a range of household cleaning products), community acceptance of their products has been

---

[4]Wangaratta is a regional city in north-eastern Victoria.

undermined by the formulation problems which were experienced with the initial version of the company's 'green' range of products, and the negative PR received.

The main problem confronting one company (the company which manufactures the UV radiation monitors) has not been merely scepticism about the product but denial of the problem. The inventor indicated that he considered the company's major failure had been their underestimation of human beings' resistance to bad news. "Our major miscalculation was that - human denial." He cited the example of his own reaction to the diagnosis of his melanoma:

> The doctor said to me: 'Look, you haven't got much chance. The statistics are against you.'
> I went into total denial, and basically I just acted normally. I didn't stop drinking a glass of wine in the evening or doing anything that I normally did. Because there is this almost medieval idea at the moment with cancer. ... Once you become a cancer victim for whatever reason (and I knew the reason: I'd been burnt to a crisp as a child), cancer is now associated with being spiritually unclean. Cancer victims are all told to go off and eat vegetables and meditate, as much as to say 'you've got cancer because you deserve it'. ... It's a medieval idea; it's extraordinary! And of course it makes no difference what you do: the survival rate's much the same. Some come out of it; some don't - generally you don't!

In the view of the inventor, this preponderance to denial really makes the whole vision of different monitoring systems (non-scientific general public monitoring) a non-event. He stated:

> What we're dealing with here is something fundamentally human: the need to *not* know. And monitoring is about knowledge: it's about taking something which you can monitor scientifically and the general public having access to that.

This whole denial problem is exacerbated by the insidious nature of the problem of sun exposure, in which the effects are long-term and in some cases (such as the recently identified contribution of UV 'A' radiation to diseases of the immune system) not obvious.

Lack of understanding of the relevant issues also affected the larger companies in the study, although the effects of this differed slightly from those on smaller companies. For example, executives from the large Australian steel manufacturing company commented that lack of understanding of environmental issues by the general community results in pressure being inappropriately directed. Contributing to this (in their view) are deliberate disinformation and simplistic presentation of information on environmental issues, resulting in false perceptions of environmental problems by the general community which may be almost irreversible. For example, the executives cited people's perceptions of mining versus agriculture: agriculture is depicted as the struggling farmer who is the backbone of the country, whereas mining is seen as the big bad profiteer which rapes and pillages the country. Another factor contributing to such false public perceptions is the visual impact of activities. People's emotions are aroused by environmental problems which may appear obvious, whereas more serious problems which are not so obvious may be ignored. This creates a distraction from the real issues which need to be addressed and, by distorting priorities, inhibits the company's ability to deal with such issues. In the view of the executives, this results in a communication gap between the technical staff of companies such as theirs, whose attitudes are based on technical facts, and the general community, whose concerns are based on emotions.

However, this view is not universal. One large overseas-based company expressed views more like those of the smaller companies, noting that a major hindrance to the 'greening' of industry is the lack of a real driving force in Australia for improvement in environmental performance by companies. An executive commented that any change which occurs is generally driven by industry, rather than by consumer groups such as occurred in Germany.

Cost of Technology/Product/Process

The literature (Elkington 1987; Hawken 1993; Jacobs 1991; Winter 1988) refers to cost-related issues as a major hindrance to the development of environmentally sustainable industry.

Among the case study companies, this has been raised by both small and large companies, and both local and overseas-based companies.

For the manufacturer of the polluted water separator, the cost of the product has affected the success of the business, as the cheapest model is priced at around $400. With the effect of the recession on farmers - the obvious initial market for the product - few are likely to outlay $400 on an item which they do not see as an absolute essential. Similarly, the cost is likely to discourage potential urban purchasers. Staff of one major water authority suggested that the designer should try to reduce the cost to around $100 in order to capture the urban market. Costs could be reduced by using a lighter gauge of steel in the manufacture of the product, but the designer is not willing to do that, as the product's life would be significantly reduced. Increased volume of production could reduce costs per unit, but again that is dependent on the availability of capital.

Similarly, high costs resulting from low volume of production have affected the company manufacturing solar energy equipment. An executive stated that, in his view, the high cost of establishing an alternative energy system based on solar power discourages many potential purchasers. This, he says, is a 'Catch 22'[5] situation, as costs could be reduced if sales were significantly increased, but such an increase is unlikely to occur while prices remain high.

Similar views were expressed by an executive from the large overseas-based company which manufactures household cleaning products. He stated that the cost of the raw materials and the technology used in the company's 'green' products is high and this forces the cost of the products up. Given consumer resistance to paying a higher cost for 'green' products than for comparable 'non-green' products, the profit margin on the company's 'green' products is low. This is exacerbated by relatively low volumes of the products being sold, resulting in correspondingly low volumes of raw materials being required and in turn translating to high costs per unit for those raw materials. Economies of scale could be achieved by increasing sales and thus increasing demand for raw materials, resulting in lower prices for those materials.

For companies which are attempting to improve their environmental management, such as the overseas-based company which manufactures a range of paper-based hygiene and toilet products, cost factors have (at times) contributed to delays in implementing necessary or desirable environmental improvements in the company's production processes.

This was confirmed by executives of the large Australian steel manufacturing company. They stated that (looked at in the short term) there is an apparent conflict between the company's primary motivation for

---

[5]'Catch 22' is defined as "a rule or condition which prevents the completion of a sequence of operations and which may establish a futile self-perpetuating cycle" (Delbridge et al 1991 p. 285).

existence (the commercial imperative - to improve the lot of the company's shareholders) and the pressures for the company to improve its environmental performance. In the view of the interviewees, improved environmental performance generally costs money, which appears in the short-term to be in direct conflict with the company's profit motive. This challenges the popular belief that improvements in environmental performance also result in increased profits - the 'win-win' theory. Moreover, within the company budget, "the environmental dollar has to compete with the safety dollar, and with every other project dollar. Therefore it is not always straightforward." However, they also acknowledged that the future profits of the company are dependent on the development of new resource projects and new facilities, and that the rights to do that are dependent on the company's record on previous developments. Therefore, although from a long-term view "good environmental business is good commercial business", in the short term there are relatively few win-win situations in both economic and environmental terms.

Cultural Issues

Among the issues identified through the case studies as hindrances to the 'greening' of industry were cultural factors (ie. factors relating to the degree to which norms and values are shared). These included both worker-related cultural issues, which were also highlighted in the literature (Denton 1994), and broader community cultural issues.

An executive from one large company noted that it had a number of long-term employees who preferred the old 'tried and true' methods and products rather than the new innovations, and that this had at times undermined worker commitment to improved environmental management. Conservatism at the market end of the process has also been a problem for the distillery operator which produces a fertiliser from the by-products of its operations, making it difficult for the company to gain initial acceptance by local cane growers for the product.

The company which manufactures solar energy equipment stated that community perceptions exist that people who use solar energy (especially in places like Victoria and Tasmania, where there is perceived to be very limited solar energy) are a bit odd. These perceptions undermine community acceptance of solar energy.

The 'different' approach to business adopted by the large overseas-based company which manufactures cosmetics and toiletries based on natural ingredients has, according to executives, drawn some derision from 'the city' (the financial sector in the UK) which has, at times, undermined the credibility of the company. In addition, the company is attacked in the media from time-to-time, which (in the view of executives) is the result of the 'tall poppy syndrome'.

Other Hindrances

A wide range of sundry issues which have hindered the success of 'green' companies have been identified through the case studies.

Actions of Competitors

Actions taken by competitors have been identified as hindrances to the successful 'greening' of several companies in this study. One small, local company has been hindered (according to its CEO) by the litigation brought by an American competitor on the basis of alleged patent infringement, resulting in the company having spent between $20,000 and $30,000 defending itself in the case. Another company - a large overseas-based company which manufactures solar energy equipment - indicated that the periodic dumping of products on the market by competitors at low prices undermines the success of companies. Yet another small local company - the company which manufactures equipment for asbestos abatement - noted that it has suffered as a result of undercutting of its prices by competitors because of an excess of asbestos removal contractors in Australia. However, the CEO expressed the view that in the long term this excess of contractors is likely to be resolved by the collapse of many of the smaller companies which are involved in the undercutting.

One small locally-based company drew attention to the influence of its competitors within the chemical industry on government policy, which disadvantages companies such as his. The CEO described the competition between small companies such as this and the large manufacturers of chemical-based detergent products as "a case of David and Goliath". In his view, these 'chemical' companies - many of them multi-national corporations - compete with small local companies on a 'playing field' which is far from level. Because of pressure brought to bear through their umbrella trade organisation (the Australian Chemical Specialty Manufacturer's Association - ACSMA), the large chemical-detergent manufacturing companies have (according to the CEO) enormous influence on Government policy. To date, governments have not required manufacturers either to remove polluting substances from their products or to bear the costs of cleaning up the environmental damage caused by their products. According to the CEO, if the cost of cleaning up the toxic blue-green algae problems, caused by phosphates in detergents, was passed on to the consumer then the cost of such detergents would rise significantly, and consumers would be made aware of the real costs of the products they use. By not requiring this, the Government is giving chemical-detergent companies an unfair price advantage in comparison with green companies such as his which already bear the costs of the point source elimination of pollution.

Government Policies

Some government policies and practices have also been cited as a hindrance to 'green' business. For example, the company which manufactures energy efficient heating systems has suffered because the policies of energy authorities (which, at the time of discussions, were government owned) were not designed for high efficiency products. Whereas a rebate was offered to commercial or industrial customers undertaking energy efficiency projects which have a payback period of two years, the savings from this product are so great that the payback period is reduced to two months, thus making it ineligible for the rebate scheme, and discouraging potential purchasers.

The CEO of another company criticised Australian higher education policy, stating his belief that the current economic rationalist approach to education, based on cost factors, has resulted in fewer of the more costly technical courses being available. There is therefore (in his experience) a shortage of people trained in specialised technical fields such as metallurgy and a corresponding excess of people trained in generalist fields such as arts. As a result, the company has difficulty in obtaining suitably qualified staff.

Lack of Supporting Infrastructure

Two companies noted that they experience difficulties relating to the lack of infrastructure to support recycling. One of the large overseas-based companies, which is located in rural Victoria, indicated that while lack of infrastructure in Australia hinders environmental performance of industry in general, it is especially difficult for companies which are not based in capital cities. For example, there are very few opportunities for recycling of waste materials in rural areas and even limited opportunities in major cities. Even when opportunities do exist in major cities, the location of the company in rural Victoria results in further disadvantage to the company and discouragement to its recycling activities because of high transport costs. This company has large quantities of waste packaging, largely from the components it purchases for its manufacturing process. Fluctuating markets for recycled cardboard and the high cost of transporting the large volume of expanded polystyrene generated by the company make it difficult and expensive to deal with the company's waste in an environmentally sustainable way. This is compounded by the lack of an adequate labelling system for plastics in Australia, which further inhibits recycling.

Lack of opportunities for recycling also acts as a barrier to the 'greening' of another of the large overseas-based companies. One major challenge confronting the company is the use of plastics in packaging. The company uses recycled high density polyethylene (HDPE) in its packaging, and is probably Australia's largest user of recycled plastic milk containers. This type of plastic has been chosen because a number of the company's formulations cannot be exposed to light, and the alternative material (PET) is not opaque. The main problem is that there is no way of again recycling the containers. Other options were considered, including use of a mixture of plastics (PET where exposure to light is not a problem, and recycled HDPE where it is). However, a choice was made to use recycled HDPE for the whole range of products (thereby providing a market for recycled milk containers), and to work with the plastics industry to close the loop in terms of developing a market for the recycled containers. To date, this has not been achieved.

Another 'infrastructural' barrier to the success of 'green' companies identified through this study is the lack of support and/or infrastructure within organisations like the CSIRO and universities for researchers to develop their discoveries and inventions beyond the laboratory or ideas stage. For example, the inventor of the sensing device for use in kilns and furnaces stated that (in his experience) researchers are expected to complete the research up to the point of publishing the paper, but then to hand it over to industry for its implementation. In the view of the inventor, this is a disincentive to the people who are doing the research, not only because their intellectual material is not bringing them any financial rewards, but also because they generally do not have the satisfaction of seeing their ideas and inventions come to fruition.

University researchers are faced (in his view) with a further difficulty in developing their ideas and inventions - the lack of infrastructure within universities. For example, the research being conducted by the inventor on heat exchangers is hindered by the lack of appropriate facilities in which such research can be undertaken. As a result, the inventor has had to find external facilities for this research (ie. a ceramics company), and has to go there to conduct this research.

Fluctuating Value of the Australian Dollar
A 'structural' impediment to three of the companies in the study has been the fluctuating value of the Australian dollar. For example, the company which manufactures the UV radiation monitors has been forced to have the card version of the monitor printed in England (because the patent for the surface coating that turns red had been bought by an English company), and fluctuations in the value of the dollar have a serious impact on the price of the cards (which are already higher in price than the market is likely to stand). The large overseas-based company manufacturing cosmetics and toiletries based on natural products also suffers from fluctuations in the value of the Australian dollar because of the significant level of importation of ingredients.

Problems relating to the value of the Australian dollar have also affected the company which manufactures erosion control and revegetation products. To establish its own manufacturing capacity (rather than sub-contracting the manufacturing), the company needs to import machinery. In the week prior to the CEO being interviewed (in September 1993) for this study, the value of the dollar had dropped to the extent that the cost of the machine in Australian dollars had risen approximately $120,000. For a small company, with limited access to capital, such a price increase is prohibitive.

Company 'Modesty'
For one large overseas-based company, 'modesty' (including the company policy of not publicising its contributions to charity and to human rights) has meant that there has been a lack of encouragement for and promotion of environmentalism both within the different sections of the company and throughout the community. According to the national sales manager, if a company promotes itself as an organisation which demonstrates serious

concern for the environment, then that requires the company to be constantly improving its environmental performance to live up to its reputation. Because this has not happened until recently in this company, there has been a risk of complacency among some employees about the company's environmental performance.

Lack of Access to Information, Assistance and Advice

For one of the small local companies, lack of access to relevant information, difficulty in gaining access to adequate evaluation of the idea and the product, and difficulty in gaining access to business advice, all hindered the company's successful initial development.

In the early stages of the product's development, a major problem was the difficulty of access to relevant information. The interviewee pointed out that many libraries are 'closed shops'. Most of the information was obtained through the chemistry library of Melbourne University, even though (in the words of the interviewee) he "was essentially an intruder" there. Difficulty was also experienced in gaining access to appropriate people to evaluate the idea for the product. The Victorian Enterprise Workshop did not offer adequate evaluation and, in frustration, the group ended up paying the Innovation Centre to undertake the evaluation. Access to businessmen, to learn from their experience, to develop business skills and to tap into their knowledge of the industry area, was difficult. Another difficulty was identifying where the product fits and therefore what industry area the group should be linking into: is it a health and safety product, or is it technical monitoring product? This has made the marketing of the product more difficult, and has contributed to the current situation of 'stagnation'.

Lack of Understanding/Commitment to the Technology

For several companies producing equipment for the agricultural market, lack of understanding of the technology and in some cases a lack of commitment to the processes necessary for its successful application have undermined the success of the companies.

The inventor of the direct tree seeding machine commented that lack of commitment to and understanding of the process of direct tree seeding including the land preparation necessary for the success of the method, by the people using it (particularly people who leased it during the trial period before it was commercialised) has undermined the reputation of the technology. He stated:

The problem at that stage was the ground preparation strategy was only poorly understood, and to give someone a machine and explain in graphic detail how the ground preparation has got to be done is actually a fool's paradise. ... Most of those people ... say: 'Oh, direct seeding has got to be easy here. Oh well, we've just finished the shearing and we won't be putting the crop in until 3.30. Oh, we've got five minutes. We'll go and put the trees in.' People that would spend half their year preparing the ground for a crop would reckon that five minutes before dinner was the right way to prepare the ground for a plantation.

Lack of commitment has undermined further the success of such plantings and the reputation of the technology within the farming community. According to the inventor, because "they didn't have the fire in the belly, they'd forget to close the gate and the cattle would spend three months in the plantation ... and then they'd sort of say 'Oh well, it doesn't work. It's the bloody machine that's wrong, you know."' By 1985, the company realised that it was making a fundamental mistake in not ensuring that people understood the importance of ground preparation and the factors which affect the success of tree plantings.

Similar views have been expressed by the CEO of company which manufactures the ultra low volume CDA spray unit. In his view, lack of understanding and acceptance of the technology by farmers poses an ongoing problem for the company. In particular, spraying under or around mature crops is viewed with distrust by many farmers. Any 'bad news story' further exacerbates the problem. The CEO cited two cases which occurred in late 1994 where crops suffered damage (fortunately temporary) following spraying with one of the company's machines. After investigation it was determined that in both cases operator error had caused the problems. However, such incidents result in negative publicity and could damage the reputation of the company and/or its products.

In the view of the CEO, the problems arise most commonly with people who buy the machines 'because it's the thing you have to have', with those who buy a machine second hand or who don't read the instruction booklet. He suggests that there are at least three waves of purchasing associated with a product such as this.

The first wave of buying in a sales campaign are the people who have either an overwhelming need to understand why it works because they've got thousands of acres, therefore they must understand the technology because there's too much at stake, or they grasp the technology straight away and understand why it works and how it works. They're no problem, they're responsible.

The next wave are people who've looked over the fence and probably understand it, and they'll take it too.

The next wave is that 'he's doing it and he's doing it, so I've got to have one'. Now he's motivated from an entirely different basis. He doesn't know why he's using it, he just knows it works. ... They're the fellows who will tip in a bit more (chemical than is necessary or safe) because they think it will work better. It's been a universal problem ever since man's been on earth - everybody seems to think that more is better.

With each wave, the understanding of the product and its functioning diminishes and the likelihood of operator error increases. The CEO believes that the company's greatest problem is in educating people, especially the second and third wave buyers (who may buy for consumerist reasons rather than environmental ones).

Landcare Program

The structure of the Landcare program has, in the view of the inventor of the direct tree seeding machine, eliminated what should (in theory) have been a primary market for his product. In the view of the inventor, the problem relates to the fact that the government funds these groups, and that groups form in order to access government funding. He is sceptical (based on his experience with a farm trees group in his own locality) about the number of Landcare groups claimed by the government to be operating, and says:

we're told that there are now 1385 Landcare groups in Australia, but see, 1292 of those have actually closed again and they're still opening more. So it's a real problem to hold interest.

In the view of the inventor, the philosophy of Landcare (that people need to be given financial help and encouragement to improve the sustainability of their land) is misplaced. He believes it would be much better to get rid of the whole Landcare infrastructure and simply get information out to farmers to enable them to ask for the help they need. He said:

I've been asked as an artist a lot of times to help people with their painting and the one thing I've learnt is that you're wasting your time if you give ten minutes to anyone who hasn't come and really asked for it.

Comparison of Literature and Case Study Data on Hindrances to the 'Greening' of Companies

The exploratory nature of this study is emphasised again by a comparison of the literature on factors hindering the 'greening' of industry with the case study data.

Case study data supports the literature in respect of a number of issues, including: difficulty gaining access to finance; variability in standards/regulations and their enforcement; the limited size of the local market; absence of an adequate environmental labelling/monitoring system; problems with government bureaucracy; skills and experience in management; cost-related issues; and worker-related cultural issues.

However, there are a number of issues raised in the case study data which do not appear in the literature. These include: the effects of the economic recession; lack of support or opposition from environmentalists, consumer organisations or other stakeholders; taxation arrangements (specific issues to do with sales tax and income equalisation); undermining of the credibility of a product or process by competitors; tariff policies; ambivalent community attitudes; and a range of other issues identified by companies in the study.

One factor which was identified through the literature - Australia's abundance of natural resources - was not noted by any of the companies in the study.

Overview of the Findings on Factors Hindering Companies

One key informant, from an organisation in Britain which promotes the development of 'green' industry, stated that there were two key problems preventing the spread of 'green' industry: the lack of will of individuals in companies, based on a lack of comprehension of the issues; and the "major structural problems" posed by the fact that companies operate within the financial world where 'environment' is seen as an 'externality' (Peckham, A. 1994, personal communication, 31 January).

The case studies, however, indicate a much broader range of factors hindering companies.

Most common among the factors hindering companies was difficulty gaining access to finance. This was particularly a problem for the smaller companies in the sample. Banks came in for a great deal of criticism about their lending policies from small companies in this study, one of which was forced out of business as a result of problems with lending institutions. The comments of several of the case study interviewees, criticising not only the policies but also the decision-making skills of bank staff (ie. drawing attention to the interrelationship of 'structure' and 'agency'), highlight the relevance of Giddens' theory of structuration to this topic.

Lack of consistency in standards and regulations and their enforcement was also identified as a common problem affecting the success of 'green' companies. This inconsistency has resulted in unfair competition from imported goods which are not required to meet the same standards, and the lack of enforcement has undermined markets for 'green' products and caused economic disadvantage to companies which have complied in comparison with those which have not.

The limited size of the local market has been compounded by several issues, including: lack of awareness of environmental issues, scepticism concerning 'green' products, and outright denial of environmental problems. Actions by competitors, including the undermining of the credibility of the product/process, and lobbying governments to ensure that policies protect existing 'non-green' businesses at the expense of 'green' businesses have compounded the problem further. Contributing further to the limitation of success of 'green' products and processes has been a culture of conservatism among workers in some companies, among those in the financial sector, and more generally in the marketplace.

The effects of the recession were also highlighted as hindering the 'greening' of industry, by drawing community attention away from environmental issues to economic ones, and by discouraging companies from spending money on new 'green' technologies. This was seen to be compounded by the comparatively high cost of some of the technologies, products and processes. Tariff policies, which expose Australian companies to competition from cheap imports produced in countries where environmental regulations are not so strict, have further exacerbated this problem.

The absence of a satisfactory environmental labelling scheme or monitoring of environmental claims, resulting in community scepticism about environmental claims, and no advantage (and thus a comparative disadvantage) for companies which produce 'green' products, was identified as another major hindrance. Several companies also drew attention to a lack of purchaser understanding of and commitment to particular 'green' products and/or processes, which undermined the success of their application and thus of their reputation (and thereby contributed to growing scepticism of 'green' products in general). This highlights the relevance of Giddens' concept of the 'duality of structure' to this topic: application of the technology in the absence of proper user understanding of and commitment to its diligent application resulted in lack of success in this use of the technology, which further undermined the understanding of and commitment to the technology.

Government policies, programs and structures have also hindered the success of 'green' industry, according to the case study informants. For example, government energy policies were said by informants to have included inappropriate conditions for rebates on energy efficient appliances, and education policies to have contributed to a shortage of technically skilled staff. Criticisms were levelled at the conditions governing grants, contracts and government-related business development schemes as being inappropriate and unnecessarily bureaucratic. However, as with banks and lending institutions, the problem has not been restricted to 'structural' issues. 'Structural' problems were seen as being compounded by an 'agency' element relating to the attitude and approach of staff of government departments which (according to one key informant) ranged from apathy to active opposition.

A range of other factors hindering the success of 'green' companies were identified through this study. They included:

- the structure of the companies themselves (including their size, organisation and staffing profile) and the nature of their business;
- lack of supporting infrastructure (such as infrastructure to support the expansion of recycling, and infrastructure within universities to develop ideas and inventions identified in universities);
- fluctuations in the value of the Australian dollar, which particularly affect companies which are involved in importing raw materials or machinery, or exporting manufactured goods; and
- lack of access to information, assistance and advice.

10 A Typology of 'Green' Companies

Introduction

Although a wide range of motivating factors for the 'greening' of industry was identified through this study, these have been grouped to provide four main 'motivational types':

- compliant;
- opportunistic;
- pragmatic; and
- ideological.

It should be noted that, whilst the classification of companies according to this typology is on the basis of the company's main motivation for 'greening', most companies have acknowledged more than one motivating factor and many have cited a range of factors. Assessment of which is the company's 'main' motivating factor has been made on the basis of the data obtained through the interviews with key informants in the companies.

Compliant Companies

Compliant companies are defined as companies which have adopted cleaner production techniques and/or produced 'green' products primarily in order to comply with regulations, community expectations and/or to avoid penalties.

Within the study sample, nine companies were deemed to be primarily motivated by compliance to regulations and/or community expectations. Seven of the nine companies in this category were included in the study sample on the basis of their cleaner production techniques, while the other two were included on the basis of a combination of cleaner production techniques and 'green' products.

All of the companies in this category have a long history of manufacturing. The majority are overseas-based companies, and all but one are classified as large companies.

Opportunistic Companies

Opportunistic companies are defined as companies with no particular inherent concern for the environment but which have become 'green' primarily because they see an opportunity for strategic advantage through cleaner production methods and/or the development of 'green' products.

Of all the categories, this one accounted for the largest proportion of companies in the sample (twelve out of the total of thirty companies). All are companies which were included in the study on the basis of the 'green' products which they manufacture. All but three are small, locally-based companies which have been relatively recently established.

Pragmatic Companies

Pragmatic companies are defined as companies which have adopted cleaner production techniques and/or produced 'green' products primarily because of their direct experience of a specific need.

Two of the companies in the sample have been classified as companies motivated primarily by direct experience of need. In both cases, they are small locally-based companies which manufacture products directed primarily at the agricultural market.

Ideological Companies

Ideological companies are defined as companies which have adopted cleaner production techniques and/or produced 'green' products primarily for ideological reasons.

Seven of the companies in the study have been classified as ideologically motivated companies. All but one are small locally-based companies which have been included in the study on the basis of the 'green' nature of the products they manufacture. The seventh company is the Australian franchise operation of a large overseas-based company which is included on the basis of both the 'green' nature of its products and the clean production processes used in their manufacture.

Case Study Examples of Company 'Types'

Case 1:   **Australian Dyeing Company**

Company 'type':   'Compliant'

Nature of business:

This company dyes cotton fabrics using a method which requires no salt and which minimises effluent.

Corporate structure:

The company is a joint venture between two families, and is a private company with 2 directors and 200 employees.

History:

The company began its operations in 1958 at Clifton Hill, and became a commission dye house for processing both knitted and woven fabrics. In 1979 a second plant was acquired in rural Victoria, enabling the rapid expansion of the business.

During the 1980s, the metropolitan plant improved its environmental performance in all areas of emissions (effluent, noise and odour), and altered its traffic and parking arrangements to take account of the needs of its residential neighbours.

However, the lower level of environmental awareness in rural Victoria enabled the company to continue its dyeing operations at its decentralised plant despite high salt levels in the plant's effluent. This effluent is discharged into the local sewerage system, from which discharges find their way into the Goulburn-Murray river system. The CEO states:

> We did not create the salt problem in the Murray, but in the twelve months to June 1991 we dumped 1,000 tonnes of salt into the Murray.

A request from the Victorian EPA to the local sewerage authority to reduce the salt content of its effluent resulted in a request by the local sewerage authority to the company to reduce its reliance on salt. The future of the plant and the company was at risk unless the company could comply with the requirements of the local sewerage authority and the EPA.

The Directors were aware of the process known as 'cold pad batch dyeing with trickle wash' which eliminates the use of salt from the dyeing process. However, this process had not been used in Australia, and specialist equipment was required to enable its introduction. To assist the company to purchase this equipment, the Directors applied to the Victorian EPA for a special grant under the 'Clean Technology Incentive Scheme'. The application was successful, resulting in partial funding of the purchase of equipment. By March 1991 the new dyeing process was in operation.

According to the CEO, the process as used by the company - cold pad batch dyeing with trickle wash, which the company has branded 'smart cotton colours' - is significantly better for the environment. It benefits the environment through:

- less chemicals - no salt, no lubricants;
- less water - up to 48% less water consumption;
- less effluent - because less water is used; and
- less energy - up to 33% less because the dyeing process does not require heat.

Motivations:

According to company sources, there were a number of factors involved in motivating the company to adopt ecologically sustainable processes in their production.

Initially, pressure from the EPA in terms of emissions from the metropolitan plant, combined with neighbour complaints to the local Council about traffic and pollution, forced the company to modify its operations. Waste minimisation in order to reduce costs was also a factor, with the company filling 12 dumpmasters each day with waste. Safety was also an issue, with overflow from the condensation tank in the plant flowing across the floor, presenting a workplace hazard as well as costing the company in wasted water.

As outlined above, it was initially also pressure from the EPA which prompted the company adopting ecologically sustainable processes in its rural plant, in the form of the cold pad batch dyeing process. However, having accepted that it would need to adopt more ecologically sustainable processes in order to meet the EPA requirements, the company realised that the adoption of such processes would also give it a new opportunity for marketing. Market research had shown that the environment is an important factor affecting consumer choice. In promoting the environmental benefits of its dyeing process, the company has been able to tap into this environmental concern.

The movement of the economy into recession was an important motivating factor too. For companies to survive in recessed economic conditions they need to be differentiated from their competitors, and this company chose to do that by adopting this new green process.

Company success:

The company has been very successful, being (according to the CEO) "the largest and most modern commission dye house in Australia". A 'Company Profile' prepared by the company states:

> (the) Company has successfully built up an excellent business in a very competitive environment and is well poised to achieve further sales increases and greater profitability.

This success, particularly in recent years, has related directly to the ecologically sustainable nature of the process, since that has been emphasised in the company's promotional material.

Factors assisting:

Internal factors:
The main internal factor assisting the company's movement into the cold pad batch dyeing process was the existence within the company of appropriate technical expertise and knowledge.

External factors:
The provision of a grant from the Victorian Government under its Clean Technology Incentive Scheme for the purchase of equipment was an important factor in the successful establishment of the new process.

As noted above, the recession aided the company in one sense by highlighting the need for differentiation.

Factors hindering:

The recession also hindered the company in some ways, as consumers became less concerned about the environmental aspects of products and more concerned about economic factors.

Government policies of reducing tariffs and quotas, and allowing an increase in cheap imports, have undermined the success of the whole textile, clothing and footwear industry, including this company.

Lack of awareness or concern in the community about the need to buy Australian made products and to buy products which are 'green' has further limited the success of the company.

Possible Government policy initiatives:

Three possible Government policy initiatives which could promote the establishment and success of green industry in Australia have been identified by this company:

- financial incentives for green production - for example, more grants such as given to this company for purchasing equipment, or grants to assist with R & D;
- import controls - particularly quotas to ensure that the number of imports is limited, giving local companies a chance to compete; and
- tighter labelling laws - to ensure that false or misleading claims are not made by companies.

Necessary conditions outside Government control:

To support the development of green industry in Australia, it is (in the view of the CEO) essential that community awareness be raised about the importance of production being 'green', for the sake of the planet and future generations. In addition, there needs to be greater community awareness of the importance of buying Australian made products.

Case 2:   **Seldco Pty. Ltd.**

Company 'type':   'Opportunistic'

Nature of business:

This company manufactures, sells and services machines which enable safe disposal of fluorescent tubes through the neutralising of sodium gases, recovery of heavy metals and separation for recycling of metals and glass.

Corporate structure:

Seldco is a private company with 3 partners and 3 part-time employees (although it formerly employed 6 people). Decision-making is undertaken jointly by the partners.

History:

Although the formal establishment of the company did not take place until 1989, the process of the development of such a product began in 1986, when one of the partners won a contract with the State Electricity Commission of Victoria (SECV) to change streetlights from fluorescent tubes to mercury vapour or sodium lights. As part of the contract, he was required to return the fluorescent tubes to an SECV depot for storage.

By the late 1980s there was increasing concern in the community about green issues. After three years of storing the tubes and having no way of dealing with them, the SECV spoke to the contractor about the possibility of developing a method of safe disposal of the tubes. In response to this, the company was formed, and was registered in November 1989.

Motivations:

In the view of the partner interviewed, environmental manufacturing is "the growth industry of this decade and probably the next". The motivation for the establishment of the company was related therefore predominantly to its potential for commercial gain. According to advertising material prepared by the company, fluorescent lamps':

> are classed as dangerous goods under the Dangerous Goods Act 1985, Act No. 10189, because they contain many substances listed in the Dangerous Goods (Prescribed List) Regulations 1986.
>
> This means these lamps must be transported, stored and disposed of in accordance with
>
> 1. The Environment Protection Act 1970 Act No. 8056 (Disposal).
> 2. Dangerous Goods (Storage & Handling) Regulations 1989 Statutory Rule No. 323 (Storage).
> 3. Environment Protection (Transport) Regulations 1987 Statutory Rule No. 193 (Transport).

In view of that, the market for a machine which safely disposes of fluorescent tubes seemed assured.

Company success:

Although the company has been successful in developing a machine capable of safely disposing of fluorescent tubes, it has been less than successful in a business sense. At the time of the initial interview, only 12 machines had been sold. Reasons for this are detailed below.

Judging by the publicity material put out by two of the purchasers of the machines, the success of the company (limited though it has been) has certainly related to the green nature of the product. The former City of Box Hill Electricity Supply Department encouraged its householders to bring their used fluorescent lamps to the Department for disposal via the machine, saying: "Remember, you'll be helping protect our environment" (City of Box Hill Electricity Supply, October-December 1991). Similarly, the former Coburg City Council urged ratepayers "to be conscious of their environment and to take advantage of this free service by not breaking their old lamps but delivering them intact ... for safe disposal in the lamp crusher" (City of Coburg, October-December 1991).

However, business nevertheless remained slow (almost static), and in 1994 a decision was taken to move the company from Melbourne to Canberra, on the basis of advice that New South Wales was likely to be much more serious in its environmental regulation than Victoria. Since then, business has generally remained slow, although there was a significant increase in the number of enquiries about the product during January 1996.

Factors assisting:

According to the partner interviewed, "nothing has assisted the company".

Factors hindering:

Impediments to the success of the business have related primarily to the failure of governments and government agencies to enforce the legislation which prompted the development of the product.

Both the Environment Protection Authority and the Victorian State Government refused in 1991 to specify methods for the disposal of fluorescent tubes, despite the fact that they contain substances classed as 'dangerous goods' under the Dangerous Goods Act 1985. In a letter dated 15th August 1991 to one of the partners of the company, the EPA Director of Policy stated:

> Until there are recovery systems which minimise the emission of mercury to air or water, the Authority is reluctant to require any particular collection or disposal method for fluorescent tubes.

According to the partner interviewed, this reluctance of the EPA to enforce the law relates to two issues:

* the EPA's preference for a single large-scale disposal facility rather than multiple smaller facilities; and
* lack of staff within the EPA to enforce the regulations.

A second factor inhibiting the success of the company has been lack of access to funds for developing local and overseas markets. Opportunities exist overseas, with disposal of fluorescent tubes in landfill sites banned in both the European Community and USA. However, the company would need agents overseas to demonstrate their product. The estimated cost of establishing such a marketing program is $250,000 - a sum which is beyond the means of the company at this stage.

The recession has also inhibited the company's development, in the view of the partner interviewed. The growing environmental concern of the late 1980s, which was seen as likely to translate into action for environmental preservation (and thus into markets for environmental products) has taken second place to economic concerns.

Possible Government policy initiatives:

In the view of the company, the enforcement of government legislation and regulations relating to the environment will be critical to the success of companies which set up in response to environmental concerns.

Government purchasing policy also is seen by the company as an important means of fostering the growth of green manufacturing companies such as this. For example, according to the company, the Education Department should be encouraged to purchase one of its machines to dispose of the 60,000 fluorescent tubes which are replaced every two years in the Rialto building.

Necessary conditions outside Government control:

No suggestions were offered.

Case 3: **Company 'C'**
(Name withheld at request of management)

Company 'type': **'Pragmatic'**

Nature of business:

This company has invented and developed a machine for direct seeding of trees, particularly designed for the planting of shelter belts on farms.

Corporate structure:

It is a private company with two shareholders and two directors (the inventor and his wife).

History:

In spring 1974 the inventor, having recently returned from six years of working overseas, was riding a horse through a grove of trees on the property which he now farms, when it struck him that the trees, particularly the red gums in Western Victoria, were thinning out. At a time when other people were taking no notice of the issue, he began thinking about the implications of a long term rural tree decline.

Initially the inventor's interest was in the long-term welfare of agriculture and its inter-dependence with the eco-system. Even now, over twenty years later, the interdependence of eco-systems and agriculture is not a popular concept.

Having identified the problem, the inventor and his wife began trying to identify the causes for the decline as well as the symptoms. They began looking at issues associated with the nutrition of trees - for example, examining what impact ground compaction had on the nutrition of trees; they tried using foliant sprays to redress nutritional imbalances; they did plant tissue analyses and soil analyses, comparing trees which had come from 'supered' (superphosphate fertilised) and 'non-supered' country.

> The basic premise we were working on was that it was going to be numbers of trees that made the difference, not so much the quality of trees, and we started to look at what the long term future for a place like ours held in terms of tree numbers. And in fact by about ... 1982 ... if you had have asked us what we thought about the future of the place, even then we would have said 'look, we need to be able to plant 380,000 trees on this place in the next ten or fifteen years to just make it environmentally stable and sustainable in the long term'.

In fact we've put in more than that - considerably more than that - and we're only about half-way, so in fact we underestimated. But the significance of the 380,000 then was that even in 1981/82 you were talking about $2.50 a tree, and it was clearly impossible financially for a farmer to withstand that sort of burden. And the other thing is that you were talking about a very very hard day to plant 200 trees. ... Quite obviously something had to be developed to bypass that problem.

Now it happened that I'd been involved even by that stage for about fifteen years in some natural regeneration - shutting blocks off and assessing what was happening with that. And we'd made some fairly scientific assessments of what the success of those had been. We had sixteen blocks we'd shut off and we just looked at the potential of that. And we decided that of the sixteen blocks, one was a total right-off (there was just absolutely nothing had come in it), one was what we termed a success, and the other fourteen were just really ... pretty mediocre. So by say 1983/84 we had a pretty fair assessment of whether natural regeneration was a reliable and efficient technique in revegetation - and it just wasn't.

Having determined that natural regeneration did not offer a satisfactory solution to the decline in farm trees, and having realised that saving the existing trees (using nutrition support methods) would be expensive and difficult and not necessarily effective, the inventor and his wife began to look for a more economical and efficient method of establishing a new generation of trees.

They settled on the idea of direct seeding, and decided to develop a specialist machine, specifically designed for direct seeding of Australian native trees and shrubs.

A syndicate of farmers was formed in 1981 to fund the prototype machine and to trial it. After ten years of trials, a company was formed to manufacture and market the machine.

Motivations:

The underlying motivation for the machine's development was the need to redress the declining sustainability of the inventor's own land, resulting from loss of trees. An article about the machine and its inventor, from 'The Weekly Times', September 9, 1992 (p.15), suggests that it was motivated by "fear of soil degradation and a lack of shade and shelter".

The problem which confronted the inventor was how to develop (not only for his own use but also for other farmers) a mechanism to establish trees where they are wanted, at low cost and at high speed.

Company success:

The company has been very successful, and is probably the leading provider of revegetation services in Australia. Recently, the company has successfully negotiated agreements to export the technology.

Factors assisting:

Internal factors:
The range of skills and interests of the inventor have been an important factor in the successful development of the machine. He is a biologist who has worked on five continents, and has an interest in natural history and ecology. That has fed his interest in the taxonomic relationships between species, which has been helpful in his revegetation pursuits. In addition, he has been for twenty-five years a professional artist, and has as a result a certain skill in the area of observation.

As well, he grew up on a farm and was encouraged by his father to observe what was going on around the farm and to understand why it was occurring. He recalls as a child driving around the farm with his father and seeing a flock of crows feeding in one corner of the property. His father would say: "I wonder what they're doing. Let's go over and see why (they're there)." They would go over and dig around to see what grubs the crows were feeding on, then try to identify the grub, work out what it would develop into and why it was there, and whether or not it was harming the pasture.

His farming background has also been important in understanding issues confronting farmers who are, after all, a major market for the product.

External factors:
The problem of lack of commitment to ground preparation by users of the machines has been overcome in recent years because nearly everyone who comes and buys a machine receives back-up consultant support from the inventor. As a result they gain a clear understanding of the technology and how it should be used, and they develop a real commitment to the whole project. An important factor in this commitment is the financial investment they have made to purchase the machine - once they have made that initial financial commitment, then they realise the value of the exercise and become committed to its success.

Factors hindering:

One of the early problems confronting the project was with the establishment of the original syndicate of farmers.

In 1981, because of the lack of awareness of or interest in the relationship between agriculture and ecosystems, it was not easy to get a group of eight farmers who were interested in a new technical system for tree planting.

Scepticism and resistance from the bureaucracy (such as the reaction of a CSIRO scientist to the seed coating used in conjunction with the tree seeder), resulting from the bureaucracy's desire to control the whole area of farm tree planting has undermined the acceptance of the concept and technology of direct tree seeding in the community. According to the inventor, "... government bodies are inevitably antipathetic to technology that gives individuals independence. Technology that enables farmers to revegetate at low cost (ie. without grants) and single handed (ie. without the assistance of a government employee) is not a vote winner in government circles. Their future jobs are contingent on maintaining farmer dependence on government assistance."

Resistance also came from a major environmental organisation which (in the words of the inventor) 'white-anted' the reputation of the machine in the major commercial markets available to the company: mining companies and forestry companies. (Interestingly, an urban arm of the same environmental organisation began negotiations with the company to purchase one of the machines. They sent people to visit the inventor and see the machine and how it worked. They took photographs and took measurements of the machine. After about eight months, when asked by the inventor what they wanted to do about it and when they wanted the machine, it emerged that they had commissioned someone to make a machine for them, having obtained the design and measurements from the inventor.)

This resistance from government departments and the environmental group made it difficult to provide potential buyers with referees who could show them large-scale examples of plantations developed using the machine.

The timing of the project, which coincided with the drought in 1982/83 and, since its commercialisation in 1991, with the recent drought and the rural recession, has also hampered the spread of the technology and therefore the company's success.

Lack of commitment to and understanding of the process of direct tree seeding including the land preparation necessary for the success of the method, by the people using it (particularly people who leased it during the trial period before it was commercialised) has further undermined the reputation of the technology. The inventor put it this way:

> The problem at that stage was (that) the ground preparation strategy was only poorly understood, and to give someone a machine and explain in graphic detail how the ground preparation has got to be done is actually a fool's paradise. ... Most of those people ... say: 'Oh, direct seeding has got to be easy here. Oh well, we've just finished the shearing and we won't be putting the crop in until 3.30. Oh, we've got five minutes. We'll go and put the trees in.' People that would spend half their year preparing the ground for a crop would reckon that five minutes before dinner was the right way to prepare the ground for a plantation.

Lack of commitment further undermined the success of such plantings and the reputation of the technology within the farming community. According to the inventor, because "they didn't have the fire in the belly, they'd forget to close the gate and the cattle would spend three months in the plantation ... and then they'd sort of say 'Oh well, it doesn't work. It's the bloody machine that's wrong, you know.'" By 1985, the company had realised that it made a fundamental mistake in not ensuring that people understood the importance of ground preparation and the factors which affect the success of tree plantings.

A further difficulty has arisen because of the structure of the Landcare movement, which should (in theory) have provided a primary market for the machine but which has failed completely to do so. In the view of the inventor, the problem relates to the fact that the government funds these groups, and that groups form in order to access government funding. He is sceptical (based on his experience with a farm trees group in his own locality) about the number of Landcare groups claimed by the government to be operating, and says:

> we're told that there are now 1385 Landcare groups in Australia, but see, 1292 of those have actually closed again and they're still opening more. So it's a real problem to hold interest.

In the view of the inventor, the philosophy of Landcare (that people need to be given financial help and encouragement to improve the sustainability of their land) is misplaced. He believes it would be much better to get rid of the whole Landcare infrastructure and simply get information out to farmers to enable them to ask for the help they need. He said:

> I've been asked as an artist a lot of times to help people with their painting and the one thing I've learnt is that you're wasting your time if you give ten minutes to anyone who hasn't come and really asked for it.

The tendency of governments to charge for services provided by Austrade makes it difficult for small companies such as this to access the benefits of association with such organisations, because of needing to pay large sums of money 'up-front'. In addition, the relevant specialised agricultural arm of Austrade known as Agrotech, to which companies such as this would be dealing, has as its directors people from companies which are direct competitors of the applicant company. Companies are loath to apply for assistance because they would be required to disclose to those directors sensitive details of the company which they would not otherwise have disclosed to their competitors.

In addition, in the view of the inventor (developed as a result of his experience in dealing with government departments and organisations such as Austrade) a major problem in dealing with such bodies is that they are often less interested in the value of the technology or project than they are in the political kudos they will gain from the publicity associated with it.

Within the company itself, a factor limiting the success of the product has been the size of the company. With only two partners, and given the wide range of other (competing) interests of the inventor and his wife - for example, he is a professional artist and runs a 4000 acre sheep station, as well as working as a consultant on revegetation - there is a limit to the amount of time and energy they have to put into marketing the machine.

Possible Government policy initiatives:

According to the inventor, the best thing the government could do would be to get out of revegetation projects. He strongly believes that the government should simply give farmers a tax break rather than grants to undertake revegetation, and should allow farmers to choose where they get their information (either from private consultants or government departments). This would put farmers back in control of the process and would be the best way of obtaining their commitment to revegetation.

In addition, the role currently undertaken by Austrade would, in the view of the inventor, be better undertaken by banks.

Necessary conditions outside Government control:

No suggestions were offered.

Case 4:	**Company 'D'**
	(Name withheld at request of management)
Company 'type':	**'Ideological'**

Nature of business:

Company "D" manufactures a laundry detergent which contains no petrochemicals, phosphates, enzymes or optical brighteners.

Corporate structure:

It is a proprietary limited company with three shareholders, two directors and four employees.

History:

The founder and CEO of the company originally trained in Applied Biology at RMIT in the late 1960s, and while studying part-time worked at the Commonwealth Serum Laboratories.

His involvement in manufacturing dates back to 1982, when with a partner (an industrial chemist) he established a company to manufacture natural-based toiletries and cleaning products. Marketed under the name 'Herbon', the products were manufactured from natural (herbal and mineral) ingredients, and excluded petrochemical ingredients. The motivation for the business was the desire to manufacture non-polluting products without animal testing. However, the company also saw a "spin off" benefit for people who suffer allergies which, according to the CEO, are more likely to occur with petrochemical based products. However, after two years in that business, the partnership failed and was dissolved.

After an absence from business for about five years, in 1989 the opportunity arose for the establishment of another business. The CEO floated the new company (Company "D"), with two major shareholders (the CEO and the second Company Director) and two minor shareholders.

Motivations:

According to the CEO, the primary motivation for the choice to be involved in 'green' manufacturing rather than any other type of manufacturing relates to his history of environmental concern.

Influenced by Rachel Carson's book 'Silent Spring' - he says "she had a very profound influence on me" - in 1969 he wrote an article for Catalyst (the RMIT student newspaper) entitled 'Pollution - the chain can break'. Later he was influenced also by Peter Singer's book 'Animal Liberation', and became actively involved in the animal liberation movement. He was on the committee of Animal Liberation for a number of years. He has therefore had a long history of involvement in both environmental and animal rights issues.

At the time when he was considering starting another business (in 1989), the CEO knew that there were no laundry detergents being promoted as phosphate-free. Therefore, in addition to satisfying the CEO's desire to care for the environment, there was seen to be a market opportunity. This was an important secondary motivation. In the words of the CEO, "quite clearly you don't go into business at the end of the day unless you feel that you can make a living out of it".

Company success:

The success of the company to date has been limited (for reasons outlined below), with the company suffering severe cash flow problems for about eighteen months from 1993 to mid 1994. Since then, the business has been 'turned around' to make a "comfortable profit". The CEO's feelings about the company's success to date are summed up in his statement that:

> there are lots of things you can put your money into, and with hindsight I wouldn't have put it into this. ... It's just been too difficult.

However, negotiations which resulted in the company having the manufacturing sub-contract with a company which has an exclusive arrangement to supply a range of 'green' products to a major supermarket chain provided a much-needed breakthrough. That success related directly to the 'green' nature of the company's own products. As the CEO stated:

> Without that, we wouldn't even have been talking to this company. So maybe having stuck in/hung in there being 'green', having persevered with it, did pay some dividends; but it certainly didn't pay any dividends for the first three years.

Factors assisting:

Given the limited success of the company to date, it is not surprising that factors which have aided the company were difficult to identify.

Internal factors:

The background of the CEO in Applied Biology has assisted with the development of products, in terms of chemical formulation. There is also an advantage in the small size of the company, and the ready availability of the second Company Director, which means that decisions can be made quickly and informally.

The launch of the cleaning products which the company was manufacturing on a sub-contract basis greatly assisted the company's cash flow because (in the words of the CEO) "as subcontract suppliers, we were able to get some good margins". However, there were problems with payments from the company for which the sub-contract manufacturing was undertaken, with the result that the range of products being manufactured under sub-contract has been reduced from three to one (a laundry powder).

Another important factor in the success of the company (in the view of the CEO) is the quality of the product. He stated:

> It is our view that if the product wasn't above all a good washing performer, the company would not now be in business.

External factors:

The securing of a loan through August Investments (an 'ethical' investment trust) has enabled some of the cash flow problems of the company to be overcome. This capital was able to be secured because of the green nature of the company's business. (However, there were also some difficulties associated with this arrangement. August Investments' involvement was via redeemable preferential interest [dividend] shares. Early in 1995, it was mutually agreed that the shares would be redeemed in full and not be converted to capital. A small dividend was paid. The redemption had the potential to severely strain cash flow, but the company was able to cope with the cash payout, which also had the benefit of maintaining greater equity for existing shareholders.)

In the view of the CEO, "the current success of the product can be attributed to the fact that the company weathered the recession storm because we were able to get the support of loyal customers who continue to purchase the powder week in-week out (regularly), despite aggressive discounting by competitors. One must remember the economies of scale of the large manufacturers allow them to offer some pretty tempting deals".

Factors hindering:

Many factors have impeded the success of the company, including:

- the impact of the recession on a fledgling business;
- the influence of the chemical industry on Government policy;
- lack of access to funds for marketing and lack of marketing skills;
- sales tax arrangements;
- shortcomings of the Environmental Choice program;
- lack of support from environmental and consumer organisations;
- lack of enforcement of regulations/guidelines on product labelling;
- slowness of action on Standards;
- Federal Government encouragement of imported products and lack of assistance to small companies to tap into exports; and
- internal disputes between shareholders and management.

The CEO described the competition between small companies such as this and the large manufacturers of chemical-based detergent products as "a case of David and Goliath". In his view, these 'chemical' companies - many of them multi-national corporations - compete with small local companies on a 'playing field' which is far from level. Because of pressure brought to bear through their umbrella trade organisation (the Australian Chemical Specialty Manufacturer's Association - ACSMA), the large chemical-detergent manufacturing companies have (according to the CEO) enormous influence on Government policy. To date, Governments have not required them either to remove polluting substances from their products or to bear the costs of cleaning up the environmental damage caused by their products. According to the CEO, if the cost of cleaning up the toxic blue-green algae problems, caused by phosphates in detergents, was passed on to the consumer then the cost of such detergents would rise significantly, and consumers would be made aware of the real costs of the products they use. By not requiring this, the Government is giving chemical-detergent companies an unfair price advantage in comparison with green companies such as Company "D" which already bear the costs of the point source elimination of pollution.

This disadvantage for small, local 'green' manufacturers such as Company "D" is compounded further by marketing problems. Unless consumers are made aware of benefits, in economic and/or environmental terms, of purchasing green products, the manufacturers of such products face an uphill battle. They are competing for market share with large corporations which have budgets of millions of dollars for television advertising. According to the CEO, lack of skills within the company in terms of management and marketing has been a problem: "I think managing a business - particularly the marketing side of things - is the hardest part. I think our business problem is a marketing problem - the biggest problem is lack of funds to market the product properly."

The CEO approached banks (including the Commonwealth Development Bank) and the Small Business Development Corporation, but had no success in obtaining funds. The only outside source of funds has been August Investments Managed Trust - an 'ethical investment trust'.

The cash flow situation of the company has been hampered not only by lack of outside funding sources, but also by Government taxation policies. The company was required to pay the sales tax on its products before it had received payment from supermarkets for the goods it had supplied.

Short-comings of the Environmental Choice program have been highlighted as a major factor in the company's problems. The company supports the concept of an independent environmental claims evaluation. The CEO believes that such an evaluation is important for the protection of consumers and of companies which genuinely want to make improvements in terms of reducing their environmental impact. However, he believes the failure of the program to make any value judgements about products has meant that companies which paid the fees and had their environmental claims verified have received little advantage. Any advantage which was received - the right to use the 'Environmental Choice' symbol on their products - became (in the view of the CEO) a disadvantage in the light of widely publicised criticisms of the Environmental Choice program by environmental, consumer and industry groups. He says:

> we were part of it, and although individually I don't think that anybody has been able to fault our product in terms of what we say about our product and what we're doing with the product, however we were guilty by association, I guess. I guess to that extent, environmental organisations probably haven't given our product very much credibility. ... So rather than helping us it probably hindered us.

This disadvantage is further compounded by the failure of the Trade Practices Commission to enforce the guidelines relating to environmental claims for marketing. As a result, companies whose claims for their products have not been verified continue to gain an unfair advantage by making dubious environmental claims. As the CEO put it:

> In other words, most consumers at the moment if they look at packaging of products would say that there is no reason for them to use our product, because we really can't say anything much more significant in terms of our environmental claims that we make about our product as compared to these products who are making environmental claims.

In the view of the CEO, the failure of the Australian Standards Association to complete its review of the standards for biodegradability of detergent surfactants (a review which has been in progress for the past six years) has also disadvantaged his company. It has meant that standards have not been changed to meet the environmental problems we are now facing, and thus other companies are able to claim that they are meeting the standard for biodegradability, when in fact that standard is inappropriate and outdated by comparison with standards set by the International Standards Organisation. This is (says the CEO) "a further example of the power of the major players".

Possible Government policy initiatives:

According to the CEO, as well as ensuring that guidelines and standards are enforced, Government should adopt a purchasing policy which is biased towards green products. Made enquiries through his local MP (a Federal minister), but he declined to see him.

Another suggestion was that Governments should impose an environmental impact tax, possibly replacing some existing taxes (such as payroll tax).

Necessary conditions outside Government control:

If the CEO had known that support from environmental organisations and their membership would not be forthcoming, he would not have gone into green production. He considers such support to be essential if small businesses specialising in green manufacturing are to be encouraged.

Conclusion

Despite the apparent functionality of the typology described above, it is acknowledged that the divisions between the categories of motivational factors are (as noted earlier) somewhat arbitrary. Whilst some companies fall clearly into one category, others could have been allocated to several categories quite justifiably. For example, the awareness of 'need' in the case of one of the 'needs-based' companies could be said to have arisen because of an ideological commitment to environmental values. Further studies based on a larger sample of companies will be needed in order to develop a typology which distinguishes more clearly between motivational categories.

Within each of the categories, there is evidence supporting Giddens' concept of the 'duality of structure'. For example, the 'carrot and stick' nature of the motivations for the 'greening' of industry is exemplified in the fact that most (if not all) of those companies which are primarily motivated by compliance are at the same time benefiting from opportunities which such compliance offers to differentiate themselves from the competition and to save on costs, thereby gaining competitive advantage. This duality further complicates the task of developing a typology with discrete categories.

11 Tips for Growing 'Greener' - Conditions Needed for 'Green' Industry to Expand

Introduction

In this age of 'quick fix' solutions to problems, a chapter which provides a list of 'handy hints' is almost mandatory for any book. When the problem being addressed is the ecological unsustainability of industry, then the need is even more critical.

But the reality is that there is no simple set of actions which can be taken by any one individual, organisation or group which will resolve the problems hindering the 'greening' of industry and facilitate its expansion. Rather, action needs to be taken at a number of levels simultaneously:

- at all tiers of government (Federal, State and Local);
- within the financial sector;
- within industry (in particular, within the manufacturing sector);
- within consumer and environmental organisations; and
- at the individual consumer level.

In addition, at each of these levels, change needs to occur in two areas:

- in relation to underlying environmental values and ethics; and
- in terms of practical actions.

Unless change occurs in *both* of these areas, resulting in actions which are based on a commitment to an 'environmental ethic', then practical actions taken to foster the 'greening' of industry are unlikely to be maintained when economic and/or political circumstances change.

Material obtained through this study and through the literature review provides the basis for the following recommendations concerning a framework for the promotion of 'green' manufacturing in Australia.

Government Actions Needed to Foster the 'Greening' of Industry

The role of governments (Federal, State and Local) in the 'greening' of industry is critical, since it is governments which largely control the political, regulatory and fiscal regimes within which industry is required to operate. Unless these regimes are conducive to the 'greening' of industry, such 'greening' will be, at best, limited. And such an integrated framework fostering the 'greening' of industry is unlikely unless governments are committed to an environmental ethic.

The Climate Change conference in Kyoto, Japan in December 1997, offered an opportunity for the Australian Government to demonstrate its commitment to the environment and to the expansion of 'green' industry. Instead, the Australian delegation argued successfully (although many Australians do not view it as a 'success') that Australia should be allowed to increase rather than stabilise or decrease its emissions of Greenhouse gases, because of its high level of dependence on fossil fuels. Many academics, economists, environmentalists and ordinary Australians argued strongly against this stance, suggesting that it was based on the views of narrow sectional interests rather than on robust economic analysis as was claimed by the Federal Government.

This recent experience in Australia indicates that, at a Federal Government level at least, there is a lack of serious commitment to an environmental ethic, resulting in a policy framework which at best does not help and at worst undermines the viability of 'green' industry. This view is supported by Diesendorf (1997), who stated in a paper presented to the Australia New Zealand Society for Ecological Economics in November 1997:

> Present government industry policies ... are attempting to hold back (the) transition to a cleaner and more efficient ... economy. (Diesendorf 1997 p. 11)

The findings of this study support that view and indicate a need for Australian governments to adopt an environmental ethic, culminating in policies which actively encourage the expansion of 'green' industry.

The following discussion outlines a range of policy areas in which governments could make changes which would foster the development of 'green' industry.

Stricter Environmental Regulation

The most important change needed at a government level is in the area of environmental regulation.

In keeping with the findings of the literature review, rather than seeing strict environmental regulation as an unmanageable burden for industry, many companies in this study expressed the view that tighter and more consistent regulation would be both a spur and an aid to the 'greening' of industry.

Informants indicated that inconsistencies in regulation governing the various jurisdictions within Australia need to be removed, that regulations need generally to be more stringent, and that they need to be more promptly and strictly enforced.

There was recognition that this would be in direct contrast with the current trend towards greater deregulation/self-regulation, and would pose problems in terms of enforcement given the current emphasis on fiscal austerity within government departments and regulatory agencies. Nevertheless, strict environmental regulation was the most frequently cited suggestion to foster the 'greening' of industry.

Regulatory Changes at Federal Government Level

At a Federal Government level the most obvious change needed is the adoption of a stringent and binding target and timetable for reduction in the level of Australia's greenhouse gas emissions.

Such an action would provide recognition to existing 'green' industries, most of which have undertaken their 'greening' with little or no government support. It would also signal to the rest of the industrial sector that the dominant (unsustainable) industry model in Australia, with its fossil-fuel dependence and its model of self-regulation, has passed its 'use-by' date and must be replaced by a new model based on ecological sustainability. This would provide both opportunity and stimulus to Australian industry to respond innovatively with new products and processes. In addition, any revenue raised through penalties or taxes for non-compliance with new regulations would provide a funding base for support of developing 'green' industries.

The *failure* to take this action would ensure the continuation of the existing unsustainable industry policy in Australia, and would discourage the establishment of new 'green' industries, with their potential to meet demand from both domestic and export markets.   With other countries adopting more stringent greenhouse gas targets, the new market opportunities created would be cornered by manufacturers in those countries, leaving Australia's manufacturing sector languishing in the past.

Regulatory Changes at State Government Level

At this level of government, the most obvious need is for collaboration between the various governments to align the relevant legislation and regulations, and to ensure consistency in enforcement policy.

Broadly speaking, environmental protection in terms of emissions to air, land and water is the responsibility of State and Territory governments. Inconsistency in the content and enforcement of environmental regulations across Australia undermines the market for 'green' products, and gives a competitive advantage in terms of reduced costs to companies which, though polluting, are not penalised.

Through the standardising of legislation and regulations, and their enforcement, 'green' companies (which would not incur penalties) would gain a comparative advantage over their environmentally damaging competitors, unsustainable companies would be encouraged to avoid harming the environment, new markets would be generated for 'clean and green' technologies and products, and innovation would be stimulated.

Regulatory Changes at Local Government Level

Local governments contribute to environmental management through local planning and environmental health laws, including bearing responsibility for waste management and disposal in local landfill sites and for overseeing building regulations, including mandatory standards for insulation.

At this level of government the need is more for change in the enforcement of regulations than in the regulations themselves.

Failure to enforce regulations, for example in respect of the disposal of fluorescent tubes, undermines the markets for products developed to fulfil those regulations. By contrast, strict enforcement of the regulations creates market opportunities at the same time as it protects local environments.

Changes in Taxation Policy

While there is a general recognition, by governments, of the importance of taxation instruments in creating an environment conducive to the establishment and expansion of industry, the specific needs of sustainable industry do not appear to have been recognised. As a result, 'green' companies are forced to compete on a playing field which is far from level, both in their competition with existing (non-'green') industries in Australia and with overseas 'green' industries for both the domestic and export markets.

Changes are needed to the overall taxation regime in Australia, including the imposition of new taxes on ecologically unsustainable business activities and the switching of subsidies from environmentally damaging activities to sustainable industries. In addition, changes are needed to the systems of taxation payment, particularly in respect of small businesses, in order to foster innovative 'green' industries. Because of the limited capacity of State and Local Governments in Australia to impose taxes, recommendations for tax reform are directed at the Federal level.

Taxation Changes at Federal Government Level

At a Federal Government level, a number of specific recommendations for changes to the taxation system emerge from the findings of this study.

The first group relates to variations in existing tax provisions. In order to encourage the adoption of 'green' technology in industry, there is a need for accelerated rates of depreciation. Rather than writing off investment in new 'green' technology over a period of seven years, companies need to be able to write it off over a two year period, in order to make the investment economically viable. Similarly, there is a need for more appropriate systems of income equalisation for small developing companies manufacturing 'green' products for specialised markets. The current taxation system does not take adequate account of the peaks and troughs in income within such companies. This limits the capacity for these companies to establish themselves on a firmer footing through reinvesting the profits in the business. There is also a need to adjust the range of business expenses allowed as tax deductions to ensure that they encourage sustainability in industry.

Another set of recommendations relates to the imposition of new taxes. In order to 'level the playing field' for companies which adopt 'green' production processes and to encourage existing industries to reduce their environmental impact, there is a need for imposition of an 'environmental impact tax', and for a tax on feedstock raw materials to reflect the environmental costs of their use and to encourage recycling. The revenue generated through these taxes could be used to support the development of further 'green' industry through the provision of subsidies, grants and loans.

Government Support for Small Business

Increased government support for small businesses is an essential element of any significant expansion of 'green' industry in Australia.

Whereas support for big business is well established, support for entrepreneurial small business is less readily available. As the literature indicates, small business is a key source of innovation in Australia, and this is true as much in the 'greening' of industry as it is in any other area of innovation. Yet Federal and State Government small business development schemes are, because of their excessive bureaucracy, ineffective in facilitating the development of those innovative ideas into secure businesses.

Both monetary support in the form of grants and equity partnerships (rather than loans), and other forms of support such as business advice forums, particularly in the initial development stage, and promotional support at the export market development stage, have been identified as requirements. It has been suggested also that the government should step in where necessary to offer short term support to small 'green' companies struggling because of poor management.

Federal Government Support for Small Business

Specific recommendations for changes in support by the Federal Government for small business include changes in conditions governing Government contracts and Government grant schemes, and legislation to facilitate increased funding for small business support programs.

Criteria for assessing tenders for Government contracts should be modified to enable appropriate small businesses to apply. For example, criteria specifying quality assurance accreditation (ISO) and minimum levels of turnover and/or profit, should be replaced by criteria based on evidence of the capacity of the applicant to fulfil the contract requirements.

Similarly, the conditions governing industry 'Research and Development' (R & D) grants should be amended to reduce the minimum annual company expenditure on R & D from $30,000 per annum to a more appropriate level for small businesses.

In order to increase the funding available to support small businesses, the money raised from import duties should be specifically earmarked for supporting local manufacturing industry. Another suggestion for funding support for small business is the introduction by the Federal Government of legislation requiring superannuation funds to invest a certain proportion of their funds in small business, receiving in return a tax deduction (as well as any dividend earned on their investment).

State Government Support for Small Business

At a State Government level, there is a need for Government grants to small business to be more substantial, with grants in the order of $5,000 to $10,000 being seen as too small to be effective. A scheme similar to the former Victorian Economic Development Corporation is needed to offer funding and other support for small business. However, such a scheme requires skilled administrators who are capable of accurately assessing the likely success of proposed ventures.

Environmental Labelling Laws

If 'green' industry is to expand then there needs to be some way for 'green' manufacturers to distinguish their products, on the basis of their ecological sustainability, from other products on the market. A comprehensive system of environmental labelling for products, based on independent testing of environmental claims, and strict monitoring and controls, is needed.

Such a scheme needs to be established Australia-wide and to be within the reach of small companies in terms of costs. The Federal Government is, therefore, the most appropriate body to implement such a scheme.

One company suggested that the independent testing should be undertaken by the CSIRO and should involve a two-stage process. An initial government grant could be made available (where necessary) to companies to pay for the CSIRO to undertake preliminary tests to determine the environmental efficacy of products. Such preliminary tests would determine whether or not further detailed tests are warranted. If not, then the cost to government would have been relatively small. The cost of further tests could be provided up-front by the government, and recouped later through company taxes and export earnings.

Import Controls

This study confirms that there is a need to limit the number of imports of 'green' products if local companies manufacturing such goods are to be established successfully.

Due to current Federal Government policies of tariff reduction, 'green' manufacturers in Australia are faced with having to compete with overseas manufacturers for a share of the already limited local Australian market. Given that the limited size of the local market already poses significant problems for 'green' manufacturers, any reduction in access to this market through uncontrolled competition from imported goods is likely to threaten the long term viability of some Australian 'green' manufacturers.

The Federal Government should examine carefully the potential impacts of changes in import regulations on Australian 'green' manufacturers. Both the timing and the extent of relaxation of import controls should be considered in terms of their impact on local market share and export potential.

Government Purchasing Policies

One potential mechanism for overcoming the problems faced by 'green' manufacturers because of the limited size of the local market is the adoption of 'pro-green' purchasing policies by all levels of Government.

Purchasing policies biased towards 'green' products (for example, towards those made from recycled materials) and 'green' technology (for example, technology which reduces energy consumption and emissions) would provide companies with a base market on which they could build their businesses, and would also set an example for other market sectors. Such policies should be couched in terms of the characteristics of the products rather than the particular brand. In this way, support would be provided for companies which are already achieving high environmental standards, but encouragement would also be given to other companies to adopt more environmentally sound designs and processes.

Other Government Policy Areas

A number of other actions by Governments were identified as necessary to facilitate the expansion of 'green' industry. They include:

- acknowledgement of relevant environmental issues (eg. water pollution) by governments and semi-government authorities, so that such issues are at least placed 'on the agenda';
- establishment by governments of targets for 'green' technology (for example, a percentage of electricity being generated by solar energy by a given time);
- development of more appropriate accounting systems (both within government and more broadly in the community) which 'internalise' the environmental costs of products and processes;
- development of a contingency legal system to enable individuals and small companies to take legal action to protect their interests without the need for large sums of money 'up-front';
- development of a more relevant and responsive education system to ensure basic literacy, numeracy and expression skills and to develop clear thinking and lateral thinking/problem solving skills;
- development and implementation of a policy within universities and the CSIRO to encourage researchers to take their discoveries and inventions through to production and marketing stages;
- establishment of a scheme for involving unemployed people in the process of research and development by paying them additional benefits (as a way of overcoming the limited funding available to support R & D, and tapping into the innovative skills in Australia); and
- provision of subsidies where necessary to support the use of 'green' products and processes.

Actions Needed within the Financial Sector to Foster the 'Greening' of Industry

While the financial sector has a much more narrowly focused role to play than that played by governments in the 'greening' of industry, it is nevertheless a critical role. Without the support of the financial sector, significant expansion of 'green' industry will be impossible.

Not only was lack of access to finance the most frequently cited problem faced by companies in this study, but it was also the one difficulty which proved insuperable. As highlighted in Chapter 9, difficulties in dealing with financial institutions caused the demise of one previously successful 'green' business.

Like governments, the financial sector appears locked into 'short-termism'. Whereas with governments the pressure comes from concern about electoral backlash in response to stringent environmental regulations, environmental impact taxes etc., for the financial sector the pressure arises from shareholders. This study demonstrates that change is needed at three levels in the financial sector: shareholders; Board; and administrators.

It is ultimately the shareholders who dictate the policies of the financial institutions, through their choice of Board members and their voting actions at Annual General Meetings. Shareholders need to adopt a longer term view and encourage Boards to invest in and lend to ecologically sustainable business ventures, even if this results in some short term reduction in profits for the financial institution. In response, Boards need to revise lending and investment policies to recognise the needs and potential of 'green' industry.

At an administrative level, new criteria for lending to and investing in developing 'green' businesses need to be established - criteria which take account not only of the established record of such businesses but also consider their future potential. Flexibility in dealings with 'green' businesses is needed also, particularly in the early development stages of the businesses when cash flow problems may threaten otherwise viable businesses. In order to achieve this, financial institution staff who deal with 'green' businesses need to be educated about the constraints affecting such businesses and the potential offered by such businesses, and need to be encouraged by senior management to take account of those constraints and potentials in their dealings with clients.

Actions Needed within the Manufacturing Sector to Foster the 'Greening' of Industry

Clearly, the 'greening' of industry will depend very much on actions taken by companies. However, as the findings of this study show, the successful 'greening' of industry is affected as much by other factors within industry as it is by management decisions to become more sustainable. Unless the manufacturing sector addresses these other issues, then the 'greening' of industry will remain limited.

Just as shareholder culture needs to change for financial institutions to fulfil their potential in supporting the 'greening' of industry, so also organisational culture within the manufacturing sector needs to change to enhance the capacity of companies to become 'green'. Companies need to foster increased worker commitment to the companies' role as 'green' manufacturers. This will be achieved by educating workers to increase their understanding of relevant environmental issues, and maximising worker involvement in company decision making.

Much of the initiative for 'green' business arises within the entrepreneurial small business sector, in which the ideas and creativity of individuals and companies are not necessarily matched by business management skills. Therefore for the potential of 'green' industry to be realised, management training and support needs to be offered to small companies to assist them to turn their ideas into reality. This could be provided through peak industry bodies, with payment for the training deferred, or by management training organisations in return for limited equity in the small business.

Actions Needed within Environmental and Consumer Organisations to Foster the 'Greening' of Industry

Increased support for 'green' manufacturers from environmental and consumer organisations and their membership is essential if sustainable industry is to be expanded.

The literature highlights the important role played by environmental groups in the 'greening' of industry. Data from the case studies confirms this, and draws attention to the equally important role of consumer organisations. Nevertheless, both large and small companies within the study sample noted that links between environmental and consumer groups and 'green' businesses could be improved further.

Environmentalists and environmental groups are seen as having unrealistic expectations both of businesses and of the community. Extremist views within the environmental movement are perceived as discouraging the general community and the business sector from taking the necessary steps to reduce environmental damage. Scepticism within the environmental movement about businesses and their motivations for 'greening', and a failure to take account of the need for businesses to make a profit, undermine the commitment of companies to the environment. A more positive approach by environmental groups, such as groups coming to companies with ideas and thoughts on how companies could become more ecologically sustainable and on potential products for 'green' manufacturers, would help develop more of an environmental ethic in companies. Similarly, community norms cannot be ignored. As one interviewee pointed out, the community is not about to give up using cars and power tools in order to protect the environment. However, they might be encouraged to use products which have fewer negative impacts on the environment. This is where consumer organisations, which provide advice to purchasers on the quality of products and services, could play their part by highlighting the environmental benefits of particular products and thereby supporting 'green' industry.

Actions Needed at an Individual Level to Foster the 'Greening' of Industry

Throughout this chapter, mention has been made of the need for various sectors to adopt an 'environmental ethic'. But just as the literature points out that "organisations do not make decisions, but individuals do" (Jackson 1982 p.27), so also the adoption of ethics by 'sectors', 'levels', 'organisations' is only an expression of the adoption of those ethics by the individual members. Therefore, for the necessary change (outlined earlier in this chapter) to occur in underlying values and ethics at a government, corporate and community level, change is needed first in values and ethics at an individual level.

Ultimately, it comes back to the individual citizen (separately and collectively) to place pressure on governments and companies to address environmental problems. Unless this occurs, markets for 'green' products and demand for cleaner production processes will remain limited and 'green' industry will be seen as an aberration rather than as the norm.

Bibliography

Abercrombie, N., Hill, S. and Turner B.S. (1988), *The Penguin Dictionary of Sociology* (2nd Ed.), Penguin Books, London

Armstrong, H. and Gross, D. (1995), *Tricontinental: The Rise and Fall of a Merchant Bank*, Melbourne University Press

Australian Bureau of Statistics (1992), *Striking a Balance! Australia's Development and Conservation*, Commonwealth of Australia

Australian Manufacturing Council Secretariat, and McKinsey and Company (1994), *The Wealth of Ideas: How Linkages Help Sustain Innovation and Growth*, Australian Manufacturing Council, Melbourne

Baden, J. and Stroup, R.L. (1991), 'Natural Resource Scarcity, Entrepreneurship, and the Political Economy of Hope', in J. Bennett and W. Block (eds), *Reconciling Economics and the Environment*, The Australian Institute for Public Policy

Baldassare, M. and Katz, C. (1992), 'The Personal Threat of Environmental Problems as Predictor of Environmental Practices', in *Environment and Behaviour*, Vol. 24 No. 5

Bandura, A. (1986), *Social foundations of thought and action: A social cognitive theory*, Prentice Hall, Englewood Cliffs, N.J.

Barbour, Ian G. (1980), *Technology, Environment and Human Values*, Praeger

Beaumont, J.R., Pederson, L.M. and Whitaker, B.D. (1994), *Managing the Environment: Business opportunity and responsibility*, Butterworth-Heinemann, Oxford

Bennett, J. and Block, W. (eds) (1991), *Reconciling Economics and the Environment*, The Australian Institute for Public Policy

Bhat, V.N. (1995), 'Benchmarking for Environmental Excellence' in *Industrial Management*, Vol. 37 No. 1, Jan.-Feb. 1995, pp. 9-11

Birch, C. (1993), *Regaining Compassion for Humanity and Nature*, New South Wales University Press

Blaikie, N. (1993), *Approaches to Social Enquiry*, Polity Press, Cambridge

Blaikie, N. and Ward, R. (1992), 'Ecological Worldviews and Environmentally Responsible Behaviour' in *Social Wetenschappen*, Vol. 35 No. 4, 1992

Blau, P.M. and Scott, W.R. (1963), *Formal Organizations: A Comparative Approach*, Routledge and Kegan Paul, London

Brown, L. (1981), *Building a Sustainable Society*, Norton, New York

Brown, M. (1995), 'Greening the bottom line' in *Management Today*, July 1995, pp. 72-78

Cairncross, F. (1991), *Costing the Earth*, The Economist Books Ltd., London

Cassell, P. (ed.) (1993), *The Giddens Reader*, The Macmillan Press Ltd., Hampshire

Catton, W. and Dunlap, R. (1980), 'A New Ecological Paradigm for Post-Exuberant Sociology' in *American Behavioural Scientist*, Vol. 24 No. 1, pp. 15-47

Christie, I., Rolfe, H. and Legard, R. (1995), *Cleaner Production in Industry: Integrating business goals and environmental management*, Policy Studies Institute, London

Clarke, A. (1995), 'The economically and ecologically sustainable future of Australia' in L. Cato (ed.), *The business of ecology: Australian organisations tackling environmental issues*, Allen and Unwin, Sydney

Commission of the European Communities (1992), *Towards Sustainability: A European Community Programme of Policy and Action in relation to the Environment and Sustainable Development*, Vol. 2, March 1992

Committee for Economic Development of Australia (1992), *Environment Protection A Global Business Challenge*, Strategic Issues Forum

Cooley, M. (ed.) (1990), *European Competitiveness in the 21st Century*, Commission of the European Communities, A Report of the FAST expert working group

Cotgrove, Stephen (1982), *Catastrophe or Cornucopia: The Environment, Politics and the Future*, John Wiley and Sons, Chichester

Coyne, J. (1993), 'Economic Concepts and Environmental Concerns: Issues Within the Greening of Business', in D. Smith (ed.), *Business and the Environment: Implications for the New Environmentalism*, Paul Chapman Publishing Ltd., London

192 *Making Things Greener*

Dabner, J. (1991), 'Taxation and the Environment', in *Greener Smarter Better - seminar on tax effective opportunities for business to meet its environmental responsibilities*, Deloitte Ross Tohmatsu and Phillips Fox

Daly, H.E. (1991), 'Sustainable development is possible only if we forgo growth', in *Development Forum*, Vol. 19 No. 5, p. 15

Delbridge, A., Bernard, J.R.L., Blair, D., Peters, P. and Butler, S. (1991), *The Macquarie Dictionary* (2nd Ed.), The Macquarie Library Pty. Ltd.

Deloitte Touche Tohmatsu International, International Institute for Sustainable Development, and SustainAbility (1993), *Coming Clean: Corporate Environmental Reporting - Opening Up for Sustainable Development*, Deloitte Touche Tohmatsu International, London

Denton, D.K. (1994), *Enviro-Management: How Smart Companies Turn Environmental Costs Into Profits*, Prentice Hall, Englewood Cliffs, New Jersey

Department of Small Business (1992), *Green Directory: A directory of 400 small firms providing environmentally positive products and services*, Victoria Press

Dickens, P. (1992), *Society and Nature: Towards a Green Social Theory*, Harvester Wheatsheaf

Diespecker, D. (1989), 'Sanity: Interpersonal/Transpersonal Strategies for Change' in T. Jagtenberg and P. D'Alton (eds), *Four Dimensional Social Space*, Harper and Row (Australasia) Pty. Limited

Dobson, A. (1990), *Green Political Thought: An Introduction*, Harper Collins Academic, London

Dunkley, G. (1992), *The Greening of the Red: Sustainability, Socialism and the Environmental Crisis*, Pluto Press Australia Limited

Dunlap, R. and Catton, W. (1993), 'The Development, Current Status, and Probable Future of Environmental Sociology: Toward an Ecological Sociology', in *Annals of the International Institute of Sociology*, Vol. 3

Dutton, J.E. and Dukerich, J.M. (1991), 'Keeping an eye in the mirror: Image and identity in organizational adaptation', in *Academy of Management Journal*, Vol. 34, pp. 517-554

Eckersley, R. (1992), *Environmentalism and Political Theory: Toward an Ecocentric Approach*, UCL Press, London

Eckersley, R. (1995), *Markets, The State and The Environment: Towards Integration*, Macmillan Education Australia Pty. Ltd., Melbourne

Ecologically Sustainable Development Working Groups (1991), *Final Report - Manufacturing*, November 1991, Australian Government Publishing Service, Canberra

Elkington, J. (1987), *The Green Capitalists: Industry's Search for Environmental Excellence*, Victor Gollancz Ltd., London

Elkington, J. and Dimmock, A. (1991), *The Corporate Environmentalists: Selling Sustainable Development: But Can They Deliver?*, SustainAbility Limited, London

Etzioni, A. (1961), *A Comparative Analysis of Complex Organizations*, The Free Press of Glencoe, Inc.

Etzioni, A. (1970), *A Sociological Reader on Complex Organizations* (2nd Edn.), Holt, Rinehart and Winston, London

Ferris, F. (1995), 'Greening your bottom line' in *American Printer*, Vol. 215 No. 1, pp. 38-42

Giddens, A. (1979), *Central Problems in Social Theory: Action, Structure and Contradiction in Social Analysis*, Macmillan, London

Giddens, A. (1982), *Profiles and Critiques in Social Theory*, Macmillan, London

Giddens, A. (1984), *The Constitution of Society: Outline of the Theory of Structuration*, University of California Press, Berkeley

Giddens, A. (1989), *Sociology*, Polity Press, Cambridge

Glaser, B.G. and Strauss, A.L. (1967), *The Discovery of Grounded Theory: Strategies of Qualitative Research*, Weidenfeld and Nicolson, London

Hanks, P. (ed.) (1979), *Collins Dictionary of the English Language*, Wm. Collins Publishers Pty. Ltd., Sydney

Hawken, P. (1993), *The Ecology of Commerce*, Weidenfeld and Nicolson, London

Hay, R.D., Gray, E.R. and Smith P.H. (1989), *Business and Society: Perspectives on Ethics and Social Responsibility* (3rd Edn.), South-Western Publishing Co., Cincinnati

Heckert, R. (1992), Personal communication, quoted in *21.C: The Magazine of the Australian Commission for the Future*, Issue 7, Spring 1992

Irvine, S. (1991), 'Beyond Green Consumerism', in C. Plant and J. Plant (eds), *Green Business: Hope or Hoax?*, New Society Publishers

Jackson, P.M. (1982), *The Political Economy of Bureaucracy*, Philip Allan Publishers Limited, Oxford

Jacobs, M. (1991), *The Green Economy: Environment, Sustainable Development and the Politics of the Future*, Pluto Press, London

Johnston, R. (ed.) (1981) *The Dictionary of Human Geography*, Blackwells, Oxford

Jones, P. (1985), *Theory and Method in Sociology*, Bell and Hyman, London

Karp, D.G. (1996), 'Values and Their Effect on Pro-Environmental Behaviour', in *Environment and Behaviour*, Vol. 28 No. 1, January, pp. 111-133

Kelly, H., (1993), *The Urban Brownies*, The Age, 9 July, p. 13

Kemp, R. (1990), 'Why not in my backyard? A radical interpretation of public opposition to the deep disposal of radioactive waste in the United Kingdom', in *Environment and Planning*, Vol. 22, pp. 1239-1258

Lam, M. (ed.) (undated), *Use Your Initiative: Enterprise Skills for the Future*, Commission for the Future, Australian Government Publishing Service, Canberra

Leighton, Tony (1992), 'Putting it All Together: Ten Trends in Corporate Environmentalism', in *Tomorrow: The Global Environment Magazine*, Vol. 2 No. 2

Lindblom, P. (1985), 'Statement to the World Commission on Environment and Development Public Hearing, Oslo, 24-25 June' in *Our Common Future*, (Australian Edition) (1990), The World Commission on Environment and Development, Oxford University Press

Lovelock, J. (1988), *The Ages of Gaia: A Biography of Our Living Earth*, Oxford University Press

MacKenzie, D. (1991), 'The rise of the green consumer', in *Consumer Policy Review*, Vol. 1 No. 2, April

Magazanik, M. (1993), *Industry calls for rethink on green laws*, The Age, 7 July p. 7

Mannheim, K. (1940), *Man and Society*, Routledge, Chapman and Paul, London

Markus, H. and Nurius, P. (1986), 'Possible selves', in *American Psychologist*, September 1986, pp. 954-969

Marsh, Ian (ed.) (1991), *The Environmental Challenge*, Longman Cheshire, Australia

Martell, L. (1994), *Ecology and Society*, Polity Press, Cambridge

Mayer, M. (ed.) (1993), 'Environment slips down the boardroom agenda', in *The ENDS Report*, No. 227, December

Mayo, M., Pastor, J-C. and Wapner, S. (1995), 'Linking Organizational Behaviour and Environmental Psychology', in *Environment and Behaviour*, Vol. 27 No. 1, January 1995, pp. 73-89

McHugh, P. (1968), *Defining the situation: The organization of meaning in social interaction*, Bobbs-Merrill, Indianapolis

McKanna, G. (1992), 'Valuable export market opens for environmental technologies', in *Financial Review*, Monday August 17, p. 55

McKinsey and Company, and the Australian Manufacturing Council Secretariat (1993), *Emerging Exporters: Australia's High Value-Added Manufacturing Exporters*, Australian Manufacturing Council, Melbourne

Milbrath, L.W. (1989), *Envisioning a Sustainable Society*, State University of New York Press

Miller, G.T. and Armstrong, P. (1982), *Living in the Environment*, International Edition, Wadsworth International Group, Belmont, California

Mills, C.W. (1940), 'Situated actions and vocabularies of motive', in *American Sociological Review*, Vol. 5, pp. 904-913

Mintzberg, H. (1983), 'The case for corporate responsibility', in *Journal of Business Strategy*, Vol. 4 No. 2, pp. 3-15

Naess, A. (1985), *Intrinsic Value: Will the Defenders of Nature Please Rise?*, Keynote Address, Second International Conference on Conservation Biology, University of Michigan, May 1985

Nash, J. and Ehrenfeld, J. (1996), 'Code Green: Business Adopts Voluntary Environmental Standards', in *Environment*, Vol. 38 No. 1, January/February

O'Riordan, T. (1981), 'Environmentalism and education', in *Journal of Geography in Higher Education*, Vol. 5 No. 1, pp. 3-18

Pappas, Carter, Evans and Koop/Telesis (1990), *The Global Challenge: Australian Manufacturing in the 1990s*, Australian Manufacturing Council

Pearce, D. (1991), 'Environmentalism and Business', in R.A. David (ed.), *The Greening of Business*, Gower Publishing Company Limited, Aldershot

Pepper, David (1986), *The Roots of Modern Environmentalism*, Routledge, London

Plant, Christopher and Albert, David H. (1991), 'Green Business in a Gray World - Can It Be Done?' in C. Plant and J. Plant (eds), *Green Business: Hope or Hoax?*, New Society Publishers

Porritt, J. (1986), *Seeing Green: The Politics of Ecology Explained*, Blackwells, Oxford

Ralston, K. (1990), *Working Greener*, Green Press, Adelaide

Report of Inquiry: Victorian Economic Development Corporation (1989), Jean Gordon Government Printer, Melbourne

Ritzer, G. (1988), *Sociological Theory* (2nd Edn.), Alfred A. Knopf, New York

Rokeach, M. (1973), *The Nature of Human Values*, Free Press, London

Ronan, C.A. (1983), *The Cambridge Illustrated History of the World's Science*, Cambridge University Press/Newnes Books

Ryan, C., Hosken, M. and Greene, D. (1990), *The Greening of the International Market: Challenges for Design and Industry Policy*, Centre for Design at RMIT, Market Intelligence Working Paper No. 1, November

Saddler, H. (1990), *Toward Toronto: Australian Technological Innovations for Efficient Energy Futures*, Commission for the Future, Australian Government Publishing Service, Canberra

Sandbach, F. (1980), *Environment, Ideology and Policy*, Basil Blackwell, Oxford

Schmidheiny, S. (1992), *Changing Course: A Global Business Perspective on Development and the Environment*, Massachusetts Institute of Technology

Schumpeter, Peter (1992), 'Green Labels: Consumers in Claims Crossfire', in *The Age* 10 June, Environment Supplement

Schwartz, S.H. (1992), 'Universals in the content and structure of values: Theoretical advances and empirical tests in 20 countries', in *Advances in Experimental Social Psychology*, Vol. 25, pp. 1-65

Shamir, B. (1991), 'Meaning, Self and Motivation in Organizations', in *Organization Studies*, Vol. 12 No. 3, pp. 405-424

Shrivastava, P. (1993), 'The Greening of Business', in D. Smith (ed.), *Business and the Environment: Implications of the New Environmentalism*, Paul Chapman Publishing Ltd., London

Smith, D. (1991), 'The Kraken Wakes: corporate social responsibility and the political dynamics of the hazardous waste issue' in *Industrial Crisis Quarterly*, Vol. 5, pp. 189-207

Smith, D. (ed.) (1993), *Business and the Environment: Implications of the New Environmentalism*, Paul Chapman Publishing Ltd., London

Stryker, S. (1980), *Symbolic interactionism: A social structural version*, Benjamin/Cummings, Menlo Park, Cal.

Thompson, J.B. (1989), 'The theory of structuration' in D. Held and J.B. Thompson, *Social theory of modern societies: Anthony Giddens and his critics*, Cambridge University Press, Cambridge

Webb, A. (1991), *The Future for U.K. Environment Policy*, The Economist Intelligence Unit, Special Report 2182, London

Welford, R. (1994), 'Improving Corporate Environmental Performance', in *Environmental Management and Health*, Vol. 5 No. 2

West, K. (1995), 'Ecolabels: The Industrialization of Environmental Standards', in *The Ecologist*, Vol. 25 No. 1, January/February

Wicke, L. (1986), *Die Ökologischen Milliarden*, Munich

Winter, Georg (1988), *Business and the Environment*, McGraw-Hill, Hamburg

Wook Lee, B. and Green, K. (1994), 'Towards Commercial and Environmental Excellence: a green portfolio matrix', in *Business Strategy and the Environment*, Vol. 3 Pt. 3, Autumn

Worcester, R. (1994), *Societal Values, Behaviour and Attitudes in Relation to the Human Dimensions of Global Environmental Change: Use of an Environmental Activist Scale*, Paper presented to the XVI IPSA WORLD CONGRESS, Berlin, Special Session 24 'Comparing Public Opinion on the Environment', 20-24 August 1994

World Commission on Environment and Development (1987), *Our Common Future: Report of the world commission on environment and development*, Oxford University Press, Oxford

World Commission on Environment and Development (1990), *Our Common Future* (Australian Edition), Oxford University Press, Australia

Yearley, S. (1991), *The Green Case*, Harper Collins, London

Yin, Robert K. (1989), *Case Study Research: Design and Methods* (Rev. Edn.), Sage Publications Inc.

Young, J. (1991), *Sustaining the Earth: The Past, Present and Future of the Green Revolution*, New South Wales University Press

Zarsky, L. (1990), 'A Sustainable Future for Australia' in *Our Common Future*, (Australian Edition), The World Commission on Environment and Development, Oxford University Press

Index

Abercrombie, N. 36, 40, 47, 48, 50, 56
ABS (Australian Bureau of Statistics)
1, 16
access to capital/finance 93, 96, 111,
116, 117-125, 154, 173
ACF (Australian Conservation
Foundation) 30, 66
ACIC (Australian Chemical Industries
Council) 68, 103
ACSMA (Australian Chemical
Speciality Manufacturers' Association
146, 174
action by competitors 116, 132, 133,
146, 154
AFCO (Australian Federation of
Consumer Organisations) 30
AMC (Australian Manufacturing
Council) 1, 127
Amoco Cadiz 82
ANOP (Australian National Opinion
Polls) survey 16
Armstrong, H. 120
ASA (Australian Standards
Association) 126, 176
attitudes to the environment/nature 9,
14-16
Austrade 105, 134, 135, 170
Australian Government 3, 179
Australia's culture of innovation 102,
111
awareness/recognition of environmental
problems 63, 64

Bacon, F. 15

Baden, J. 96, 97, 111, 117, 125
Baldassare, M. 71, 89
Bandura, A. 61
Barbour, I. 7, 8, 14-21
Beaumont, J.R. 10-12
benefits of product/process 93, 98, 99
Bennett, J. 28
Bhat, V.N. 61, 80
Bhopal 65, 106
Birch, C. 2, 14, 20, 21, 28-30,
Blaikie, N. 20, 47-50, 54, 56, 57, 71,
78
Blau, P.M. 57
Body Shop (The) 69
Boettinger, H. 12
Brown, L. 25
Brown, M. 65, 67, 69, 80-82, 98, 102
Brundtland, Gro Harlem 27
Business Charter for Sustainable
Development 67
Business Council of Australia 67

Cairncross, F. 73, 78, 82, 103, 106
Carson, R. 17, 172
Cartesian-Newtonian science 16
case study method 50-52
Cassell, P. 41, 48
Catton, W. 38, 39
CEDA (Committee for Economic
Development of Australia) 3, 27, 130
Centre for Design, RMIT 52
Christie, I. 67, 73

Clarke, A. 97, 108
Clean Technology Incentive Scheme
   105, 160
Commission of the European
   Communities 4, 125
commitment of key staff 93, 97
community
   attitudes 119, 140-143
   awareness of environmental issues
     102-104
Conservation International 69
consumer demand 71
Cooley, M. 4
corporate
   competition 73, 74
   environmentalism 70
   environmental policies 66-68, 82-84
   image 84, 85, 87
   'modesty' 149, 150
cost
   of technology/product/process 119,
     143-145, 154
   savings (through waste minimisation,
     resource recovery and recycling)
     79, 80, 159
Cotgrove, S. 18
counterculture/1960s and 1970s culture
   20, 93, 99, 100
CSIRO (Commonwealth Scientific and
   Industrial Research Organisation)
     132, 148, 168, 190, 186
cultural issues 119, 145, 146, 154
Coyne, J. 136

Dabner, J. 130
Daly, H.E. 29
decision making in organisations 11-
   13, 189
deep ecology 20, 21, 24
Delbridge, A. 144
Deloitte Touche Tohmatsu International
   73

Denton, D.K. 11, 12, 70, 74, 78, 79.
   97, 107, 145
Department of Small Business 32, 52
Descartes, R. 15
Dickens, P. 34-6, 38-40, 45, 46
Diesendorf, M. 179
Diespecker, D. 15, 16
DITAC (Department of Industry,
   Technology and Commerce) 111
Dobson, A. 20, 25, 26
Dow Chemicals 72
Dunkley, G. 3, 25, 29, 30
Dunlap, W. 38, 39
Du Pont 68, 74, 88
Dutton, J.E. 13

Eckersley, R. 24, 125
Ecological Paradigm (sociology) 25,
   26
ecolabelling/environmental labelling
   31, 116, 131, 132, 154, 160, 184
ecologism 20, 21, 25, 26, 30
economic
   benefits 78
   climate/pressures 102, 107, 108
   economic problems 1, 2
Ehrlich, P. 17
Elkington, J. 63, 65, 66, 69, 72, 74, 78,
   80, 81, 84, 85, 98, 99, 102, 103, 107,
   125, 129, 143
employee influence on corporate
   environmentalism 70, 71
Enlightenment (The) 15
Enterprise Workshops 102, 150
environmental
   actions needed within environmental
     and consumer organisations 188,
     189
   environmental accidents 65, 66
   environmental awareness/concern of
     CEO 80-82, 87

Environmental Choice (labelling
program) 30, 31, 52, 131, 132, 174,
175
environmental damage 2, 3, 28, 45
environmental economics 28
environmental ethic 189
environmental sociology 35, 44, 45
environmentalism 20, 21, 25, 26
environmentalists
influence of 66
EPA (Victorian Environent Protection
Authority) 85, 126, 127, 158, 159,
163, 164
Cleaner Production Loans 105
ESD (Ecologically Sustainable
Development) 1, 28, 29
Working Groups 1, 27, 32
ethics 8, 68, 189
ethnomethodology 35
Etzioni, A. 57
Export Market Development Grants
134
Exxon 75
Exxon Valdez 65, 75

factors assisting the 'greening' of
industry 93-115
factors hindering the 'greening' of
industry 116-158
Ferris, F. 69, 81
financial sector actions needed 186,
187
fluctuations in the value of the
Australian dollar 149, 155
full cost accounting 64, 65

Gaia 24
Gas and Fuel Corporation (Victoria)
104
GDP 1
General Motors 68

Giddens, A. 35, 39-49, 55, 90, 91, 114,
156, 157, 182
Glaser, B.G. 54
government
bureaucracy 119, 133-135, 155
policies 147, 155, 160, 174, 185, 186
purchasing policies 164, 185
support (general) 102, 104-106
support for small business 183, 184
Greenhouse 3, 45

Hanks, P. 8, 108
Hawken, P. 4, 95, 96, 108, 130, 143
Hay, R.D. 97
Heckert, R. 74
Husserl, E. 37

ICI Company 68
import controls 161, 185
individual actions needed 189
industrial era paradigm 15
influence of environmentalists 66
Institute of Business Ethics 68
International Chamber of Commerce
67
IoD (British Institute of Directors) 9
Ironbridge (UK) 45
Irvine, S. 74, 78, 107
ISO (International Standards
Organisation) 112, 126, 133, 176

Jackson, P.M. 11, 189
Jacobs, M. 75, 82, 106, 143
Johnston, R. 21
Jones, P. 47, 48
Judaeo-Christian belief 15

Karp, D.G. 9
Kelly, H. 17
Kemp, R. 59
Kyoto (Japan) Climate Change
Conference 179

lack of
  access to finance 116, 117-125, 154
  access to information, assistance and
    advice 150, 155
  supporting infrastructure 147, 155
  understanding of technology 150-
    152, 155, 168
Lam, M. 111
Landcare 140, 152, 169
legal liability 74, 75
legislation/regulation/licensing
  conditions 102, 106, 107
Leighton, T. 5, 29, 30, 63-73, 75, 78,
  80-82, 88, 89, 97, 99, 102, 103, 106,
  107, 129
Leopold, A. 8
limited size of local market 116, 127,
  128, 154
Lindblom, P. 34
links with other organisations 102, 103
Lovelock, J. 24, 25

MacKenzie, D. 3, 131
Magazanik, M. 133
Mahoney, R. 65
Mannheim, K. 59
manufacturing sector actions needed
  187
market opportunity/competitive
  advantage 78, 79
Markus, H. 61
Marsh, I. 62, 64, 66, 102, 125, 129
Martell, L. 37, 38
Marx, K. 41
Marxian theory 35, 39, 45
Maslow, A. 8
Mayer, M. 9
Mayo, M. 13
McHugh, P. 61
McKanna, G. 3
McKinsey 95, 97, 98, 117, 127, 133,
  136

methodology 47-58
Milbrath, L.W. 21, 24
Miller, G.T. 44
Mills, C.W. 59
Minimata (Japan) 18
Monsanto 65
MORI 71
motivations
  general 59-62
  for the 'greening' of industry 62-92
Mintzberg, H. 63

Naess, A. 21
Nash, J. 67, 102
National Industry Extension Scheme
  104
natural sciences-social sciences
  dichotomy 36

organisational culture 10, 11
O'Riordan, T. 21, 23

PACIA (Plastics and Chemical Industry
  Association - formerly ACIC) 68,
  103
Pappas, Carter, Evans and Koop/Telesis
  95, 139
parent company
  influence of 82-84
Pearce, D. 70, 97
Peckham, A. 153
Pepper, D. 15, 21, 37
personal experience of need for
  product/process 85-87
Phenomenology 35, 37, 48
Plant, C. 30, 32
Plotkin, M. 69
Porritt, J. 25
Post-Industrial paradigm (sociology)
  17, 29

prior activities of organisation/company
93, 99
Project Marketing Loans Scheme 105

Ralston, K. 111
RAPS (Remote Area Power Supply)
scheme 105
recession 116, 128, 129, 154, 160, 164,
173, 174
recycling 79, 80
regulation 72, 73
stricter environmental regulation
164, 180
variability in 116, 125-127, 154
regulatory changes
at Federal Government level 180
at State Government level 181
at Local Government level 181
resource recovery 79, 80
Responsible Care program 68, 103
Ritzer, G. 35
Roddick, A. 69
Rokeach, M. 7
Ronan, C.A. 15
Ryan, C. 71, 72, 78, 82, 106

Saddler, H. 98, 127
Sandbach, F. 17-19
Schmidheiny, S. 2, 67, 68, 70, 82, 88,
97, 102, 133
Schumpeter, P. 30, 31, 131
Schütz, A. 56, 57
Schwartz, S.H. 9
SECV (State Electricity Commission of
Victoria - now Electricity Services
Victoria) 102, 104, 110, 162
senior management commitment 68,
69
serendipity 102, 108-111, 115
Shamir, B. 59-62, 70
shareholder influence 193

Shrivastava, P. 12, 13
Small Business Development
Corporation 134, 175
Smith, D. 63, 66, 73, 79, 80, 82, 98
Somerville, H. 65
structuration theory 34-46, 48, 49
structure/functioning of company 93,
96, 119, 136-140, 155
Stryker, S. 61
support from environmental/consumer
organisations 116, 129, 130
sustainable development 29
Suzuki, D. 64
symbolic interactionism 35

tariff policies 119, 136, 154
taxation
arrangements 116, 130, 131
policy 181, 182
Thompson, J.B. 41
Torry Canyon 18, 19
TPC (Trade Practices Commission)
125, 175
Transpersonal ecology 24
Tricontinental 120
typology 56, 57

Union Carbide 75

values 7-10, 60, 61
VEDC (Victorian Economic
Development Corporation) 134, 194
Victorian Government 32, 160, 163

Walpole, H. 108
waste minimisation 79, 80
WCED (World Commission on
Environment and Development) 2,
27-29, 34
Webb, A. 11

Weberian social theory 35
Welford, R. 66, 71, 78, 80, 82, 103
Werner and Merz 75
West, K. 31, 131
Wicke, L. 64
Winter, G. 3, 4, 7, 27, 64, 74, 82, 90, 98, 103, 143
Wook Lee, B. 63, 64

Woolard, E. 68, 88
Worcester, R. 9, 71, 78
World Council of Churches 28

Yearley, S. 37
Yin, R. K. 50, 51, 53
Young, J. 24

Zarsky, L. 27